GLORIOUS
CROSS STITCH

Instructions for this project are found on page 111.

GLORIOUS CROSS STITCH

Chris Rankin

A Sterling/Lark Book
Sterling Publishing Co., Inc.   New York

Editor: Carol Taylor
Art Director: Sandra Montgomery
Production: Elaine Thompson, Sandra Montgomery
English Translation: Networks, Inc.
Editorial Assistance: Nola Theiss

Library of Congress Cataloging-in-Publication Data
Rankin, Chris.
   Glorious cross stitch : more than 50 stunning projects for
every room in your home / Chris Rankin.
     p. cm.
   "A Sterling/Lark book."
   Includes index.
   ISBN 0-8069-0291-4
   1. Cross-stitch--Patterns.   I. Title
TT778.C76R35   1992
746.44'3--dc20

10 9 8 7 6 5 4 3 2 1

A Sterling/Lark Book

First paperback edition published in 1994 by
Sterling Publishing Company, Inc.
387 Park Avenue South, New York, N.Y. 10016

Produced by Altamont Press, Inc.
50 College Street, Asheville, NC 28801

Photos and instructions © Ariadne/Spaarnestad, Utrecht, Holland
English translation © 1993 by Altamont Press

Distributed in Canada by Sterling Publishing
℅ Canadian Manda Group, P.O. Box 920, Station U, Toronto,
   Ontario, Canada M8Z 5P9
Distributed in Great Britain and Europe by Cassell PLC, Villiers House,
   41/47 Strand, London WC2N 5JE, England
Distributed in Australia by Capricorn Link (Australia) Pty Ltd.
   P.O. Box 6651, Baulkham Hills, Business Centre, NSW 2153, Australia

Every effort has been made to ensure that all the information in this book
is accurate. However, due to differing conditions, tools, and individual skills, the publisher cannot be responsible for any injuries, losses,
and other damages which may result from the use of the information
in this book.

Printed in Singapore

Sterling ISBN 0-8069-0291-4 Trade
           0-8069-0292-2 Paper

TABLE OF CONTENTS

INTRODUCTION

~

Cross stitch is one of the most popular needle crafts in history. From seventh-century Egyptian textiles to the famous wall hangings worked by Mary, Queen of Scots…from the peasant costumes of eastern Europe to the flowing robes of the Middle East…from contemporary Scandinavian designs to modern American handicrafts—cross stitch has captured the imagination of everyone who loves needlework.

Why this universal affection? Perhaps it's the disarming simplicity of working with a single stitch: one diagonal thread crossing another to form an X. Perhaps it's partly the shape of the stitch itself—this intersecting of two equal lines, a symbol so instinctive to us that it appears in virtually all human codes, from hiero-glyphics to the Romance languages to the pirate maps of childhood fantasy ("treasure buried here").

Perhaps it's the variety of items cross stitch can be used to decorate, or the array of different looks obtainable from the same simple stitch with only tiny vari-ations in technique: solid masses of color versus thinly etched lines, minute flecks of thread versus assertive slashes of yarn.

Whatever the source of cross stitch's popularity, *Glorious Cross Stitch* offers you more than 50 elegant opportunities to enjoy it: samplers and sun dresses, blouses and backpacks, towels and pillowcases. Taken together, the projects are an invitation to stitch your own chap-ter in the history of this well-loved craft.

Instructions for this project are found on page 46.

~ CROSS STITCH: THE BASICS

Instructions for this project are found on page 115.

Even-weave cotton with 28 threads per inch (2.5 cm).

A supremely simple technique, cross stitch involves only a few tricks of the trade.

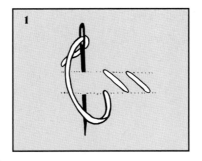

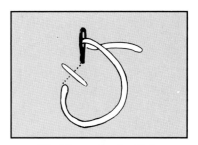

Working a single stitch.

❖ THE CROSS STITCH

Cross stitches are usually worked in rows. Working in one direction—let's say, from right to left—lay down the threads that slant the same way. Then work back along the row from left to right, adding the intersecting arms.

On the other hand, when you're working individual stitches scattered here and there, it makes sense to complete one stitch at a time. Working stitch by stitch is also useful in a diagonal row.

Regardless of how you choose to work, the upper stitch should always cross the lower in the same direction, to produce a polished, neat piece of work. If the stitches cross in different directions, the light will reflect off them differently. (As an exception to the rule, if there's a part of the design you want to particularly emphasize, you might switch directions on purpose in that area.)

❖ FABRICS

Cross stitch is a form of counted thread embroidery—that is, the actual warp and weft threads of the fabric are used to position the stitches. Each cross is made over an intersection of threads.

This imposes two requirements on your fabric. First, you must be able to *see* the threads well enough to count them. Second, you must have even-weave fabrics—that is, fabrics with the same number of warp and weft threads per inch (2.5 cm). On non-even-weave materials, cross stitches are distorted. Since they don't cross the same number of threads vertically and horizontally, they aren't square.

Any even-weave fabric will do. Various types of linen, for example, have single intersecting threads. Hessian is

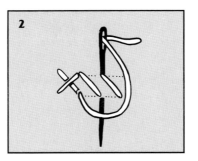

Working a straight row of cross stitches.

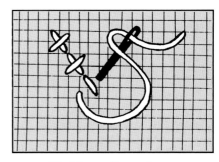

Working a diagonal row.

a coarse, inexpensive even-weave fabric suitable for such things as tote bags. At least two specialty fabrics are widely used for cross stitch. Hardanger cloth has intersecting pairs of threads; Aida cloth has intersecting groups of threads.

❖ USING THE CHARTS

In cross stitch charts, each square represents one cross stitch—or, in other words, one intersection of warp and weft threads. The symbols on the chart represent colors of yarn, which are

Aida cloth with 11 thread groups per inch (2.5 cm).

identified in the "Key to Chart." On the charted ducks below, for example, the dots represent white, the X's represent yellow, and the Z's stand for orange.

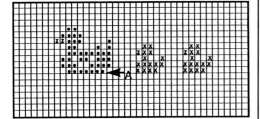

To begin work, first find the center of the fabric (fold it end to end, then side to side) and mark both centerlines, using basting thread or tailor's chalk. Make sure the center of the chart corresponds to the center of the fabric, so that the cross-stitched area doesn't end up falling off the side of the fabric.

Before beginning, always check to see how many strands of floss are prescribed and how many threads of fabric are crossed with each stitch.

❖ VARIATIONS

Although the basic stitch remains the same, the appearance of cross-stitched work can vary substantially, depending on several factors.

Stitch size. With any given fabric, the size of the stitch depends on the number of threads you are crossing. Stitches that cross six threads are obviously bigger than stitches that cross only two. Thus designs are adaptable in scale to some extent. The more threads you cross, the more of the fabric remains exposed behind the stitches, and the less solid the mass of color.

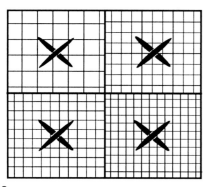

Ready-made items with strips of cross stitch fabric attached. Clockwise, from top left: an oven mitt, a baby's bib, and two hand towels.

Fabric weave. Let's say the directions tell you to work each stitch over three threads. If your fabric has relatively few (that is, relatively fat) threads per inch, crossing three of them will get you a substantial stitch. On the other hand, if the fabric is densely woven with a lot of fine threads per inch, crossing three of them isn't going to make much of an impact.

Number of strands. Working with two or three strands of floss creates a thicker, bolder stitch than working with a more delicate, single strand.

❖ ALTERNATIVES TO EVEN-WEAVE YARDAGE

Occasionally, even-weave fabric isn't available or isn't appropriate for a particular project. A child's backpack needs to be made of something sturdier than linen, and sewing an entire jacket of Hardanger cloth may be impractical. There are several alternatives.

Decorative bands. Craft shops and fabric stores carry spools of even-weave fabric—long strips an inch or two (2.5 to 5 cm) wide. These bands can be cut to length, cross-stitched, then sewn to sheets and pillowcases, towels and curtains, shirts and dresses.

Manufactured items. Also available are household linens and clothing accessories that have small pieces of cross stitch fabric attached, ready for decorating: terrycloth towels with borders of

Hardanger cloth, purses and carryalls with rectangles of Aida fabric; glasses cases, tote bags, and a host of others.

Scraps of fabric. The only part of a project that requires an even-weave fabric is the area that will actually be cross-stitched. Let's say you want to add the flags of several nations to a canvas backpack. One option is to tack a piece of even-weave fabric over the area where the flags will be, then work the motif through both thicknesses of fabric: the even-weave patch and the canvas backpack. When the design is complete, fray the edges, of the cross stitch fabric and trim away the excess, cutting as close to the edges of the design as possible.

Scrap canvas. Another strategy for working on uneven-weave fabrics is to create a temporary grid

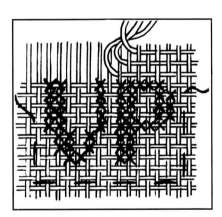

with needlepoint canvas. Select a fine, single-weave canvas (avoid interlocking meshes) and baste it to the fabric where the cross-stitched design will be. Using the canvas as a grid, work the design over the mesh and the fabric both. When you're finished, remove the basting and trim the canvas close to the embroidery, being careful not to cut the cross stitches. Then dismantle your grid. Starting from one corner, carefully draw out all the strands of canvas in one direc-

tion, then all the strands running in the other direction.

Gingham. Checked gingham is popular for cross stitch because a grid is printed on the fabric. Stitches can be worked over the colored squares, which means there's no need to count threads. The size of the stitches depends on the size of the checks.

❖ NEEDLES

Cross stitch uses tapestry needles—big-eyed and blunt. The large eye can accommodate multiple strands of floss, and the blunt tip is easy to insert between the threads of the fabric without piercing them, which is the idea in cross stitch (and in making the optional openwork hems shown on some projects). The larger the fabric weave, the larger the needle that's appropriate. A packet of assorted sizes (20 to 24, for example) should handle most fabrics. (The larger the number, the smaller the needle.)

❖ THREADS

A wonderful array of embroidery flosses are available and useful for cross stitch: stranded cottons, pearl cotton, soft cotton, wool, metallic, stranded cottons, and synthetics, among others.

Two widely available brands of embroidery floss are DMC and Anchor. For each project in this book, the key to the chart not only suggests the colors to be used but lists the product number of each color for one or both companies. Other brands (and other colors, for that matter) may be substituted. Just look for the brand's equivalent of "light gray."

❖ EMBROIDERY HOOP

An embroidery hoop holds the fabric taut while you work and helps produce unpuckered results. A hoop consists of two wooden or plastic rings, one fitting inside the other. The outer ring has an opening that can be tightened or loosened by means of a screw.

To mount the fabric in a hoop, first

place the fabric over the inner ring, then press the outer ring down around the inner one. Adjust the fabric so that it's smooth and taut, then tighten the screw to make the unit secure.

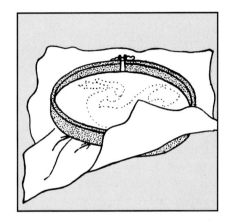

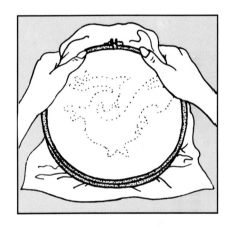

❖ STARTING AND STOPPING

Avoid knotting the floss when beginning or ending a length of yarn. To start a new strand, lay a "tail" of floss across the back of the fabric and stitch over it with the first few cross stitches. To end a strand, run the floss underneath several stitches and clip off the excess.

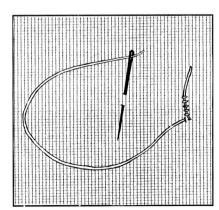

❖ ADDITIONAL STITCHES

Although all of the projects in the book use primarily cross stitch, a few other common embroidery stitches appear occasionally as accents.

Back Stitch. One of the simplest and most common outline stitches, the back stitch can be used in any of the projects that call for outlining, even if another stitch (for example, stem stitch) is specified in the directions.

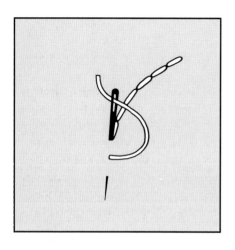

Bring the needle to the right side along the design line, take a small stitch backward, and bring the needle to the right side again in front of the first stitch, a stitch length away. Continue along the design line, always finishing the stitch by inserting the needle at the point where the last stitch began.

Stem Stitch. Stem stitches are used for strong, definite outlines

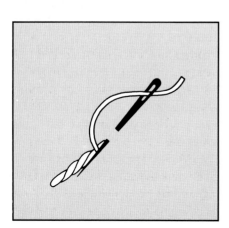

and, most commonly, for the stems of flowers and leaves (hence the name). Working along the design line, bring the needle to the right side of the fabric. Insert the needle along the line to the right, then bring it back out half a stitch length back.

Satin Stitch. Popular for filling solid areas of color, satin stitches should be flat and even. Bring the needle to the right side at the

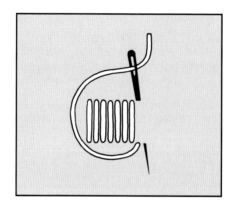

lower edge of the band to be covered. Insert the needle directly above its previous exit point, and pull the thread through.

French Knot. French knots are raised and round, and thus appear prominently as the centers of flowers and the eyes of various creatures. Begin by bringing the needle to the right side. Hold the thread taut with one hand and, with the other, wrap the thread

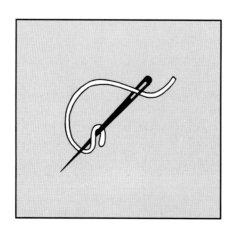

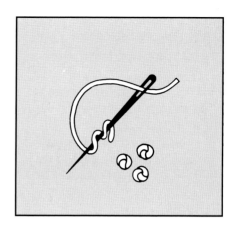

around the point of the needle twice. Pull the thread tight around the needle and insert the needle where it came out, holding the thread taut to form a clean knot. For larger knots, add more twists of thread around the needle.

Running Stitch. Bring the needle to the right side and work from right to left, picking up the same number of threads for each stitch. If the fabric isn't too heavy, you can pick up several stitches on the needle before pulling the thread through.

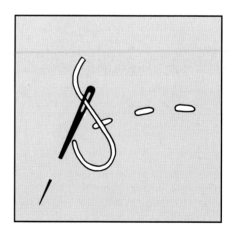

❖ MAKING MITERED CORNERS

Whether you're dealing with a sampler, a tablecloth, or a pillowcase, if it has corners, they can become lumpy blemishes on your careful work. Or they can be smooth, flat, and neat. Much as a woodworker miters corners on a well-built table, you can miter corners on your fabric work. It helps to visualize how mitering works if you fold up a piece of paper, pretending that it's fabric.

Step 1. Fold 1/4" (1 cm) of fabric to the wrong side, for an inner hem. (Whatever your outer hem, a 1/4" inner one will work.)

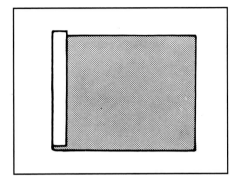

Step 2. Fold over the outer hem and press it down, to form a crease. Open the outer hem, leaving a folded inner hem and an ironed crease where the hemline will be.

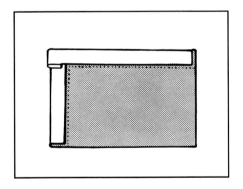

Step 3. Fold over a corner so that its fold line passes through the point where two pressed creases intersect, and iron in place. Leaving a 1/4" seam allowance, cut off the corner.

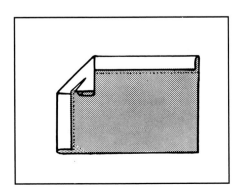

Step 4. On one edge, turn over the outer hem along the pressed crease. Pin in place.

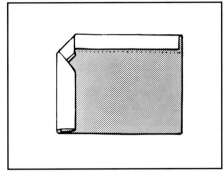

Step 5. Fold the outer hem along the pressed hemline. The two edges will meet to form a diagonal seam at the corner. Pin the corner in place, and sew up the diagonal seam with a slipstitch.

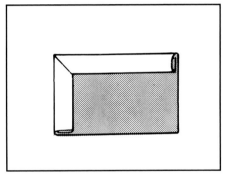

❖ OPENWORK HEMS

Several of the household linens shown in a later chapter have openwork hems, a decorative touch that is delightful but strictly optional. If you want to omit the openwork hem, the project will be complete.

To make an openwork border, first

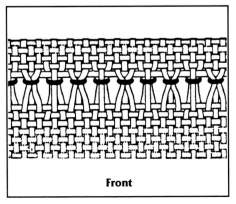

Front

find a horizontal thread the desired distance from the top of the hem. Thread a needle with the desired color, and use the needle to wrap the thread around two to four vertical threads of the fabric.

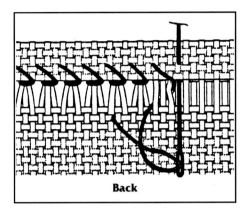

Back

Pull tightly. Continue across, carefully following the horizontal thread. You may have to adjust the number of threads to make the corner holes fall exactly at the corners. When sewing the actual hem of the piece, you may want to wrap the hemming stitches around the openwork stitches as well.

❖ CLEANING AND PRESSING

Because it will be handled extensively, a cross-stitched piece can get fairly dirty by the time it's finished. Even the cleanest hands produce some body oils.

If both the fabric and the floss are washable, treat the piece like any other delicate laundry. Just swish it around in cool, soapy water and rinse. Roll it carefully in a towel to blot up the excess moisture and lay it flat to dry. If the fabric and the floss are not washable, take the piece to a reliable dry cleaner.

The piece will need to be pressed, to remove wrinkles and any distortions in the shape of the fabric that may have occurred during the stitching. Pad the ironing board with a layer or two of towels, lay the piece face down, and cover it with a soft press cloth. If the piece has been washed and is still damp, use a dry press cloth; if the piece is dry, use a damp cloth. Press very lightly over the cross-stitched area, letting the iron just touch the cloth. Press the surrounding fabric in the usual way.

CHINA SAMPLER

✄ **Finished Measurements**
10-3/4" x 14" (27 x 35 cm)

Materials
20" x 22" (50 x 55 cm) of Flemish linen with 28 threads per inch (2.5 cm); DMC or Anchor embroidery floss as indicated on the chart; a matching frame.

Directions
Work the motif in cross stitch, following the chart and using two strands of floss over two threads. Begin at the lower right corner with the brown basket, 5-1/4" (13 cm) from the edge.

Using one strand of floss, stem stitch in and around the baskets and pots in brown; in and around the pink flowers in red; in and around the yellow flowers in orange; in and around the salmon flowers in melon; in and around the green leaves in dark green. Work the remaining stem stitches in royal blue.

Frame the finished sampler.

KEY TO CHART

Symbol	Color	DMC	Anchor		Symbol	Color	DMC	Anchor
·	= white	white	1		\	= dark green	910	230
N	= melon	351	11		\	= light green	989	240
o	= light pink	776	25		7	= green	988	242
∷	= salmon	3708	31		/	= pale pink	819	271
Λ	= pink	893	33		∅	= yellow	727	295
✳	= red	666	46		◡	= soft yellow	745	300
I	= soft blue	800	128		H	= light orange	722	323
◣	= dark blue	796	133		⬜	= soft orange	3341	328
✖	= royal	820	134		●	= orange	3340	329
+	= light blue	799	140		⌐	= pale orange	754	336
×	= blue	798	142		◣	= brown	898	360
◡	= gray blue	809	145		=	= beige	738	361
⬚	= light sea green	563	203		◹	= light gray	3072	397
V	= sea green	562	205		◢	= gray	318	399
∴	= pale sea green	955	206		▬	= ochre	729	890
⋌	= grass green	702	226		◿	= ecru	712	926
X	= dark grass green	701	227		▬	= light gray blue	932	976

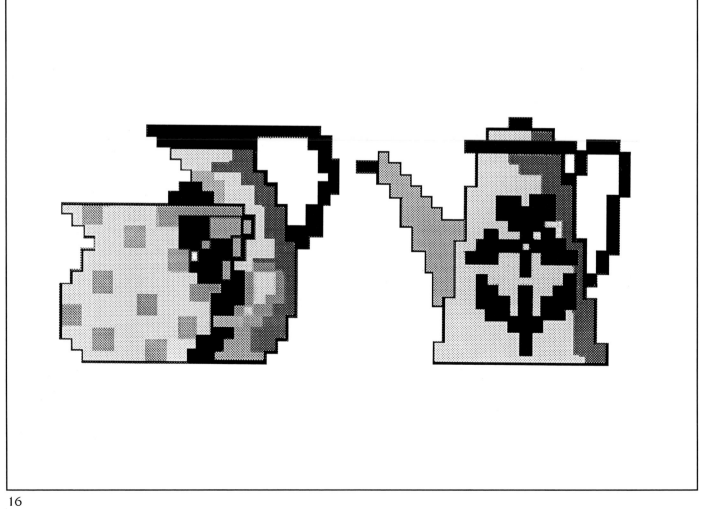

SAILING SHIPS

~

✂ Finished Measurements
17-1/2" x 20-3/4" (44 x 52 cm)
✂ Motif Measurements
14-1/4" x 17-1/2" (36 x 44 cm)

Materials

26" (0.65 m) of white linen
64" (160 cm) wide with 28
threads per inch (2.5 cm);
DMC or Anchor embroidery
floss as indicated on the
chart; a matching frame.

Directions

Cut a piece of linen 26" x 30"
(65 x 75 cm). Embroider the
ships in cross stitch, stem
stitch, and satin stitch by following the chart. Begin the
embroidery at the lower right
edge with point A, 6-3/4" (17
cm) from the right edge and
6-1/4" (16 cm) from the lower
edge (a long edge). Using
two strands of floss, work
each stitch over two threads.
Where two colors are given
on the chart, use one strand
of each color

For the black stem stitches,
use one strand of floss. For
other stem stitches, use two
strands of floss. Refer to the
picture for stem stitch colors.

Use two strands of floss for
the satin stitches. Highlight all
light rust sails with white, and
all white/gray and gray/white
sails with dark gray; but on
the boat at right center, work
the satin stitches in black.
Work the ropes in running
stitch over two cross stitches.
Frame the finished picture.

19

KEY TO CHART

		DMC	Anchor
⊡	= white	white	1
N	= dark red	304	47
●	= black	310	403
◣	= dark gray	317	400
V	= gray	318	399
‖	= rust	355/758	5975/868
▢	= light rust	356/758	883
△	= dark brown	400	351
7	= light gray	415	234
▨	= brown	434	365
⊤	= light brown	436	362
⌐	= brown gray	453	231
+	= red	666	46
╱	= beige	738	361
·	= light beige	739	885
◠	= orange	740	316
◡	= salmon	758	868
⊞	= dark blue	796	133
◹	= blue	799	145
		= light blue	800	144
�	= green	910	230
⋰	= orange brown	921	339
◥	= light orange brown	922	349
☰	= gray blue	932	343
⋋	= dark orange	946	332
∠	= yellow	973	290
X	= medium brown	976	803
O	= light green	989	242
•	= dark green	991	217

WINDOW WITH RED FLOWERS

~

✄ Finished Measurements
17-1/4" x 21-1/4" (43 x 53 cm)

✄ Embroidery Measurements
12-3/4" x 13-1/2" (32 x 34 cm)

Materials

26" (0.65 m) of white linen 56" (140 cm) wide with 25 threads per inch (2.5 cm); DMC or Anchor embroidery floss as indicated in the chart; a matching frame and mat.

Directions

Cut a rectangle of white linen 26" x 30" (65 x 75 cm). Embroider the chart in cross stitch. Embroider a rectangle in light gray 8" (20 cm) from the lower edge (a narrow side) and 6-3/4" (17 cm) from the right edge (a long side).

Using two strands of floss, work each cross stitch over two threads, but embroider the light gray wall, the white sill, and the wall with one strand of floss.

Using two strands of floss, stem stitch along the outside square with soft green; the inside square of the frame with blue; the wall in yellow brown; and along the blue area in dark gray. Work the remaining stem stitches in a shade to match the neighboring cross stitches or in one shade darker.

KEY TO CHART

Symbol	Color	DMC	Anchor
·	= white	white	1
∅	= brown	301	349
✗	= dark gray	317	400
●	= soft green	320	216
Z	= rose brown	356	5975
▲	= medium green	367	210
∪	= gray	415	398
⊠	= light brown	435	365
◿	= pale brown	437	362
◢	= dark green	501	878
◺	= green	502	876
◹	= light green	503	875
⊡	= pale green	504	213
X	= blue	518	168
+	= light blue	519	167
◉	= dark fuchsia	601	59
⊘	= fuchsia	603	57
⊿	= pink	605	55
◖	= orange red	606	334
◺	= orange	608	332
■	= dark gray brown	611	898
◸	= gray brown	612	903
⊡	= yellow brown	680	888
⊘	= light yellow brown	729	887
⊐	= yellow green	734	945
o	= yellow	744	301
⟋	= light rose brown	758	868
◿	= pale blue	775	282
◣	= dark brown	801	359
◤	= dark gray blue	930	922
✳	= gray blue	931	921
T	= light gray blue	932	920
)	= light soft green	966	206
⬓	= soft orange	3340	329
◺	= light soft orange	3341	328
◢	= dark moss green	3345	263
⊞	= moss green	3346	817
◿	= light moss green	3347	266
⟋	= very light moss green	3348	264
◺	= dark rose red	3705	28
◡	= rose red	3706	33
⟋	= pale rose red	3708	31

CHART FOR WINDOW WITH RED FLOWERS

CHRISTMAS PICTURES

✂ **Frame Measurements**
9" x 10-1/2" (22.5 x 26.5 cm)
9" x 10" (22.5 x 25.5 cm)
8-1/4" x 9-1/4" (21 x 23 cm)
8" x 10-1/4" (20 x 26 cm)

KEY TO CHARTS

		DMC	Anchor
·	= white	white	1
◢	= dark brown	300	352
/ or \	= dark red	304	47
∴	= light gray	415	234
T	= brown	436	362
=	= red	666	46
X	= dark green	699	923
V	= medium green	701	227
\	= light brown	738	361
—	= beige	739	276
I	= light shrimp	758	868
◣	= orange brown	921	339
+	= yellow	973	290
L	= green	989	225
⧄	= shrimp	3778	337

Materials

For each picture: 12" x 14" (30 x 35 cm) of white Flemish linen with 28 threads per inch (2.5 cm); DMC or Anchor embroidery floss as indicated on the chart; a frame.

Directions

Embroider each picture in cross stitch, centering the chart. Using two strands of floss, work each stitch over two threads. Using two strands of floss, stem stitch around the white/light gray Christmas ball with one strand of black #310 or #403, and around the red bow in dark red #815 or #20. Stem stitch around the shrimp colored pots in dark red brown #355 or #341, and around the brown pot in medium brown #434 or #365.

Use two strands of red to outline each motif. Outline the motif with three trees and the tree with the bow above it in stem stitch. Outline the other two motifs in cross stitch. Work the border around the motif with three trees eight threads from the lower edge and 12 threads from the top edge, with 10 threads between the outside stitch and the side edges. Work the border around the tree with the bow above, beginning six threads from the lower and side edges and four threads from the outer cross stitch. Work the border motif around the tree with the two balls, beginning eight threads from the lower edge, 16 threads from the side seams, and 10 threads from the outer stitches. Work the border motif around the two trees, beginning six threads from the lower edge, eight threads from the right side, and 10 threads from the outer stitches. Frame the finished pictures.

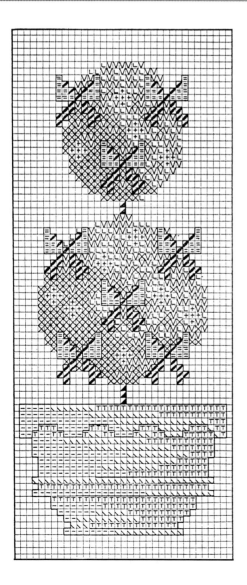

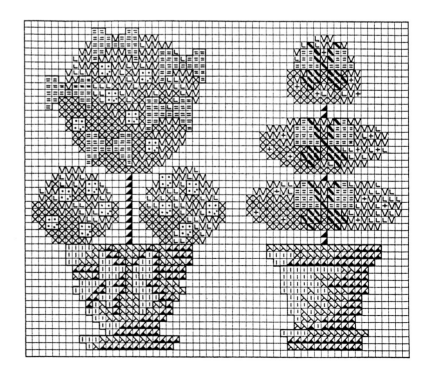

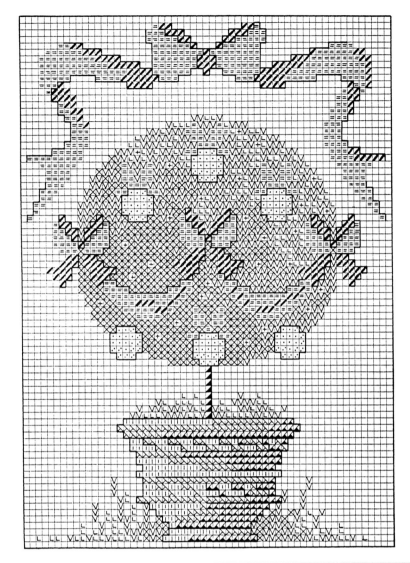

BABY SAMPLER

~

✂ Frame Measurements
21-1/2" x 25-1/4" (54 x 63 cm)
✂ Embroidery Measurements
18-3/4" x 22-1/4" (47 x 56 cm)

Materials
30" (0.75 m) of white linen
56" (140 cm) wide with 25
threads per inch (2.5 cm); DMC
or Anchor embroidery floss as
indicated on the chart, plus red
#666 or #46, dark blue #797 or
#133, and orange #970 or
#316; a matching frame.

Directions
Cut the linen in a rectangle 30"
x 34" (75 x 85 cm). Embroider
the sampler in cross stitch, stem
stitch, satin stitch, and French
knots, beginning 5-1/2" (14 cm)
from the lower right edge.

Use two strands of floss
worked over two threads for
each cross stitch. Outline in
stem stitch, using two strands
of floss. Work the patchwork
border in stem stitch, using one
strand of floss. Embroider the
eyes and nose on the large
bear, and the nose of the yellow bear, in satin stitch, using
two strands of dark gray. For
the mouth of the yellow bear
and the mouths of the small
bears, embroider in satin stitch
using two strands of orange
floss. Embroider the eyes of the
yellow bears and bear in patchwork in French knots, using two
strands of dark gray floss.
Embroider the child's name in
medium blue between the
small salmon flowers, and the
birth date in light blue, following the alphabet and numbers.

Use two strands of red floss to form a square around the name, spaced four to six threads from the name. Separate the month and birth date with a heart embroidered in blue at the same height as the year.

Stem stitch with red floss around the pink rabbit, around the pink/white hearts, and around the dark salmon/white hearts. Stem stitch around the blue hearts, in and around the blue rabbits, in and around the checked bear, and around the blue flowers with medium blue. Stem stitch in and around the patchwork border with dark blue. Work the remaining stem stitches in orange.

Frame the finished sampler.

KEY TO CHART

		DMC	Anchor
·	= white (3 strands)	white	1
◣	= dark salmon (2 strands)	350	11
●	= salmon (2 strands)	352	9
|	= light salmon	353	6
■	= dark gray	413	236
/	= light brown	437	362
⊘	= turquoise	518	161
+	= light turquoise (2 strands)	519	160
7	= green	704	238
◗	= light orange	722	323
⌐	= beige	739	361
⌐	= dark yellow	743	305
—	= yellow (2 strands)	745	292
⋰	= pale blue	775	128
◢	= medium blue (2 strands)	798	132
X	= light blue (2 strands)	809	130
⋰	= light pink	818	271
X	= blue	826	162
/	= dark pink	956	40
v	= pink	957	26

SHIRT WITH BEAR

~

✂ Finished Motif Measurements
3-1/4" x 3-1/4" (8 x 8 cm)

Materials

A white T-shirt; 4-3/4" x 4-3/4" (12 x 12 cm) of linen with 20 threads per inch (2.5 cm); DMC or Anchor embroidery floss as indicated on the chart, plus dark blue #797 or #133, but substitute dark salmon for salmon #352 or #9, and substitute black #310 or #403 for dark gray; basting thread.

Directions

Pin the piece of linen to center front of the T-shirt, 1" (2.5 cm) from the neck edge. Embroider the bear motif from the Baby Sampler in cross stitch, working through all thicknesses. In following the chart, use black instead of dark gray and dark salmon instead of salmon. Using three strands of floss, work each stitch over two threads. Stem stitch around the bear using two strands of dark blue. For the mouth, use three strands of black for the stem stitches. For the nose, use three strands of black for the satin stitches. Unravel the edges of the linen and trim away the excess.

KEY TO CHART

		DMC	Anchor
·	= white (3 strands)	white	1
◤	= dark salmon (2 strands)	350	11
●	= salmon (2 strands)	352	9
I	= light salmon	353	6
◪	= dark gray	413	236
/	= light brown	437	362
0	= turquoise	518	161
+	= light turquoise (2 strands)	519	160
7	= green	704	238
✎	= light orange	722	323
⌡	= beige	739	361
⌐	= dark yellow	743	305
—	= yellow (2 strands)	745	292
∴	= pale blue (2 strands)	775	128
◖	= medium blue (2 strands)	798	132
X	= light blue (2 strands)	809	130
∴	= light pink	818	271
✕	= blue	826	162
/	= dark pink	956	40
v	= pink	957	26

HYDRANGEAS

~

✂ Finished Measurements
19-1/2" x 22-1/4" (49 x 56 cm)

✂ Embroidery Measurements
10-3/4" x 13-1/2" (27 x 34 cm)

Materials

28" (0.7 m) of white linen 56" (140 cm) wide with 25 threads per inch (2.5 cm); Anchor embroidery floss as indicated on the chart, plus dark rose #69, blue #132, spruce #218, and dark brown #889; a matching frame.

Directions

Cut a piece of linen 28" x 30" (70 x 75 cm). Embroider the motif in cross stitch, following the chart and using two strands of floss over two threads. Where two color numbers are given, use one strand of each color. Begin embroidery at the right corner at point A, 8-1/4" (21 cm) from the lower edge (long side) and 9-1/2" (24 cm) from the right side. Using two strands of floss, stem stitch along the edges of the baskets in dark brown #889. Use spruce #218 along the leaves, blue #132 along the lilac flowers, dark rose #69 around the rose flowers, and flannel gray around the white flowers.

Frame the finished picture.

KEY TO CHART

		Anchor			Anchor
·	= white	2	⊡	= medium brown	373
▬	= pale pink	48	⋀	= warm brown	379
◣	= dark pink	65	∴	= cream	386
╱	= light rose	74	⋯	= light beige	387
╲	= rose	76	H	= light taupe	392
⁄	= purple	99	◍	= dark taupe	393
⦦	= white/ pale lilac	2/108	⊞	= gray	400
◪	= light lilac	109	✳	= dark gray	401
◡	= lilac	110	◩	= beige	830
●	= dark lilac	112	⌐	= light moss green	842
✗	= light blue	131	▽	= mauve	869
⌐	= seafoam	213	◢	= dark mauve	871
◺	= spruce	218	◣	= light brown	874
X	= green	227	◢	= hunter green	879
◥	= bright green	238	⌒	= tan	886
▱	= grass green	239	◺	= light mustard	887
⋰	= light green	241	◥	= old gold	891
◹	= medium green	243	◠	= light gray	900
⟋	= lime	253	⊘	= ochre	907
o	= dark lime	255	▲	= dark green	923
⟆	= celery	259	◺	= plum	970
◿	= brown	365	●	= flannel gray	8581

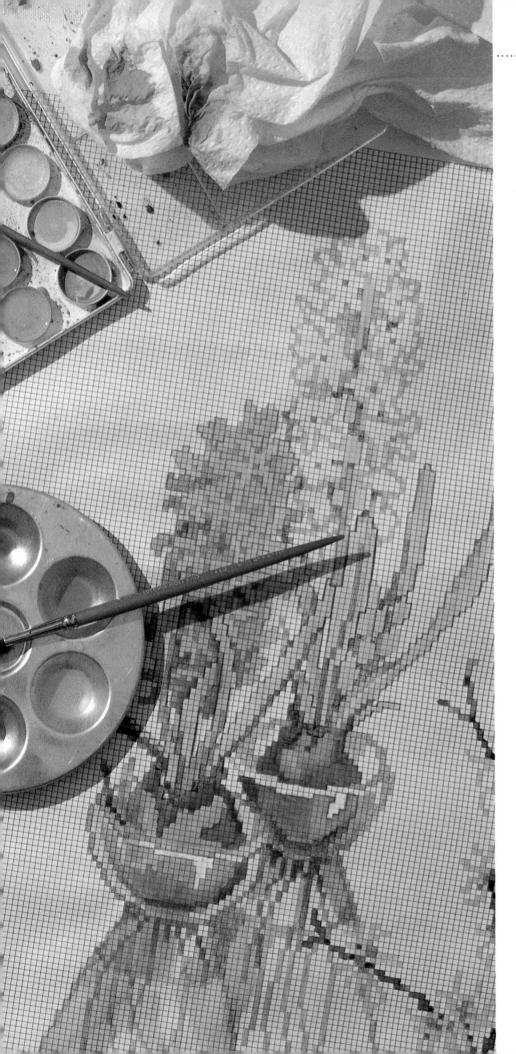

WINTER HYACINTHS

~

✂ Finished Measurements
10" x 16" (25 x 40) cm

Materials
18" x 24" (45 x 60 cm) of white linen with 25 threads per inch (2.5 cm); DMC embroidery floss as indicated on the chart; a matching frame.

Directions
Embroider the motif in cross stitch, following the chart and beginning at the lower right edge 4" (10 cm) from the edge. Using two strands of floss, work each stitch over two threads. Embroider the shadows in the glass with one strand. Using one strand of floss, stem stitch around the pink hyacinth with dark pink #601. Work the remaining stem stitches in the color of the neighboring cross stitches or in one shade darker. Frame the finished picture.

CHART FOR WINTER HYACINTHS

KEY TO CHART

			DMC
−	=	light pink	605
∅	=	pink	603
I	=	pale blue	828
=	=	light blue	800
⟍	=	blue	799
⊙	=	dark blue	798
·	=	white	white
⟍	=	ecru	746
⟍	=	gray	762
L	=	lilac	211
◖	=	purple	553
V	=	yellow	744
X	=	dark yellow	741
◢	=	dark green	905
⊙	=	yellow green	703
⬟	=	green	471
/	=	light green	472
∴	=	light gray green	504
X	=	gray green	368
··	=	light brown	738
v	=	brown	436
■	=	dark brown	420
C	=	shrimp	758
●	=	rust	356
✕	=	dark rust	355

FISH SAMPLER

~

✂ Finished Measurements
28-3/4" x 28-3/4" (72 x 72 cm);
green border: 18-1/2" x 18-1/2" (46 x 46 cm)

Materials
38" (0.95 m) of white Hardanger cloth 60" (150 cm) wide with 22 double threads per inch (2.5 cm); DMC or Anchor embroidery floss as indicated on the chart, plus green #992 or #221; matching frame.

Directions
Cut Hardanger cloth 38" x 38" (95 x 95 cm). Embroider the green square in satin stitch following the chart, beginning 9-1/4" (23 cm) from the lower and right sides. Baste the square using one strand of green floss, then embroider over the basting stitch in satin stitch, using two strands of green floss and working each stitch over two double threads.

Embroider the fish in cross stitch, using two strands of floss over two double threads. Outline the fish in stem stitch as indicated on the chart, using one strand of black floss.

Embroider the shells in cross stitch. Center the motif at point M, allowing 58 double threads below the square. Repeat the motif on all four sides. Frame the finished sampler.

KEY TO CHART

			DMC	Anchor
·	=	white	white	1
−	=	medium yellow	307	289
■	=	black	310	403
X	=	medium gray	317	400
⊠	=	dark red	347	20
\	=	red	349	19
⧄	=	dark salmon	350	13
⋈	=	salmon	351	11
+	=	light salmon	352	9
▲	=	rust	355	341
⊠	=	dark gray	413	401
V	=	gray	414	235
⧄	=	turquoise	518	168
H	=	gray green	523	859
\	=	pink	603	62
⊥	=	light pink	605	60
∪	=	golden yellow	676	891
⁕	=	dark green	701	227
∩	=	light green	704	237
⋮	=	ecru	712	590
7	=	dark pumpkin	721	324
=	=	pumpkin	722	323
∧	=	light orange	741	314
⌐	=	pale pink	754	778
⊂	=	old rose	760	36
\	=	soft green	772	259
N	=	medium blue	798	132
●	=	dark brown	801	359
C	=	light blue	809	130
◢	=	dark blue	820	134
z	=	blue	826	978
●	=	brown	839	360
⬜	=	light brown	841	378
L	=	pale brown	842	933
/	=	dark orange	900	333
◤	=	orange brown	921	339
∷	=	green gray	926	838
⧄	=	light green gray	927	848
⧄	=	silver gray	928	234
●	=	dark gray blue	930	922
◣	=	gray blue	931	781
⋉	=	light gray blue	932	343
∴	=	flesh color	945	881
Ƶ	=	orange	947	330
∴	=	pale rose	963	23
o	=	yellow	972	303
L	=	medium brown	3032	832
⧄	=	pale plum	3042	870
I	=	light yellow	3078	292
⧄	=	melon	3705	35

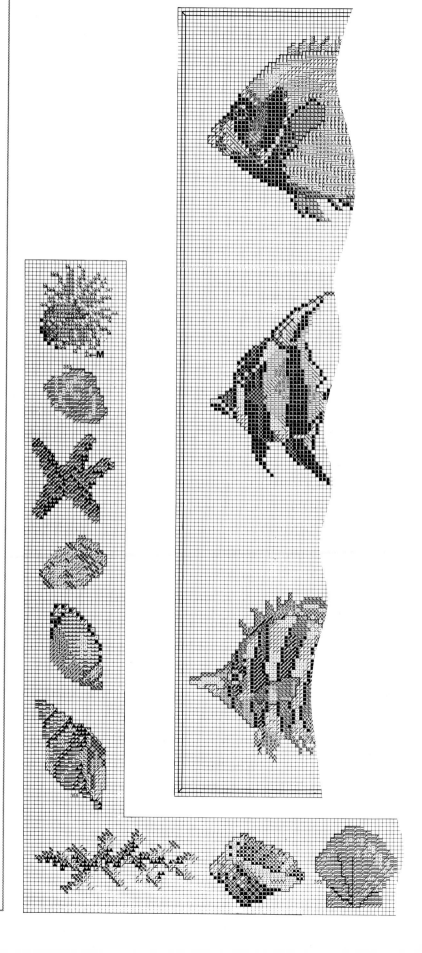

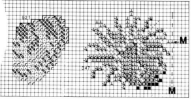

Teddy Bears

~

✂ **Finished Measurements**
16-1/2" x 23-1/4" (41.5 x 58.5 cm)
✂ **Embroidery Measurements**
10-1/2" x 19-1/4" (26.5 x 48.5 cm)

Materials
26" (0.65 m) of white linen 56"
(140 cm) wide with 25 threads
per inch (2.5 cm); DMC or
Anchor embroidery floss as
indicated on the chart; a matching frame.

Directions
Cut a piece of linen 26" x 32"
(65 x 80 cm). Embroider the
motif in cross stitch, stem stitch,
and satin stitch, beginning at
the lower right corner at point
A, 6-1/4" (16 cm) from right
edge and 9-1/2" (24 cm) from
lower edge.

On the blue gray back-
ground, work each cross stitch
over two threads using two
strands of floss. On the blue
green background, work each
cross stitch over two threads
using one strand of floss.

Using one strand of floss,
stem stitch in and around the
bear with the pink shirt with
milk chocolate; in and around
the two outside bears with
khaki; in and around the bear
with blue pants with moss
green; in the green shirt of the
bear on the background with
dark green; and around the
eyes in dark gray. Work the
remaining stem stitches in
dark brown.

Work the satin stitch mouths
using two strands of dark gray.
Frame the finished picture.

KEY TO CHART

		DMC	Anchor
· = white		white	1
∴ = ecru		ecru	275
⌣ = medium gray		318	399
⌣ = dark rose		335	38
▽ = light blue		341	117
◊ = light rust		356	5975
◣ = moss green		370	855
II = light moss green		372	853
✳ = dark gray		413	401
◺ = gray		415	234
+ = honey brown		435	365
7 = light brown		437	362
V = medium green		471	266
− = light blue green (1 strand)		598	167
∧ = yellow brown		676	891
⅄ = pale brown		677	886
A = green		703	238
∵ = yellow		727	293
◥ = dark beige		739	885
⌐ = soft yellow		745	292
∴ = pale yellow		746	386
∪ = shrimp		758	868
⊥ = light green		772	259
↗ = blue		793	121
/ = brown		840	379
o = rose		899	26
	= pale gray (1 strand)		928	847
X = dark blue gray (1 strand)		931	921
\ = blue gray (1 strand)		932	343
● = dark brown		975	351
◖ = dark green		988	257
S = dark blue green (1 strand)		991	189
= = blue green		992	186
◿ = khaki		3032	832
⌐ = light yellow brown		3047	886
Γ = yellow		3078	292
T = light rose		3326	24
⅂ = pale blue		3756	158
∷ = beige		3770	276
Y = milk chocolate		3772	883
⌐ = flesh		3774	778

A

POPPIES

~

✂ Finished Measurements
17-1/4" x 21-1/4" (43 x 53 cm)
✂ Embroidery Measurements
13-1/4" x 17-14" (33 x 43 cm)

Also shown on page 6.

Materials

26" (0.65 m) of ecru linen 56" (140 cm) wide with 25 threads per inch (2.5 cm); DMC or Anchor embroidery floss as indicated on the chart, plus blue green #958 or #187; light green fabric paint; paint fixative; a matching frame.

Directions

Cut a piece of linen 26" x 30" (65 x 75 cm) and paint it light green. Treat it with paint fixative. Embroider the motif in cross stitch and stem stitch, beginning 6" (15 cm) from the lower and right edges. Using two strands of floss, work each cross stitch and stem stitch over two threads.

Around the light brown sections, stem stitch in light ochre. Around the wheat, stem stitch with one strand of light green over two or four threads, but make the first two stem stitches with one strand of dark green. Stem stitch around the white flowers with one strand of gray; around the light sections of the rose with one strand of orange red; around the dark sections with one strand of red; in and around the centers of the flowers with one strand of black. Work the dots in French knots. Work the stem stitches of the leaves and stems in green. Work the remaining stem stitches with one strand of floss in colors matching the neighboring embroidery or in one shade darker.

Frame the finished picture.

KEY TO CHART

		DMC	Anchor
·	= white	white	02
■	= black	310	403
◖	= lilac	340	118
╱	= light salmon	353	08
◣	= dark moss green	367	217
∷	= gray	414	399
N	= brown	435	365
O	= yellow	444	291
∧	= yellow green	472	253
▼	= plum	550	101
◺	= dark green	561	211
X	= green	562	209
L	= light green	563	208
╱	= orange red	606	335
⌐	= light brown	676	891
✗	= red	817	47
⌣	= pink	899	40
—	= pale green	966	206
V	= light ochre	977	363
⌀	= orange	3340	329
▢	= light orange	3341	328
v	= light moss green	3348	259

TREASURES FOR TEA TIME

~

✂ Finished Measurements
18-3/4" x 20-1/4" (47 x 51 cm)

✂ Embroidery Measurements
14-3/4" x 16-1/4" (37 x 41 cm)

Materials

26" (0.65 m) of white linen 56" (140 cm) wide with 25 threads per inch (2.5 cm); DMC or Anchor embroidery floss as indicated on the chart, plus dark blue #797 or #147; a matching frame.

Directions

Cut linen to 26" x 28" (65 x 70 cm). Using two strands of floss over two threads, embroider the motif in cross stitch by following the chart. Begin at the lower right corner 5-1/2" (14 cm) from the edge. Embroider inside the red and blue border lines in ecru. Using two strands of floss, stem stitch in and around the darker colored teapots, the cups and the smaller sugar bowl on the left with dark blue #797 or #147; the remaining teapots, cups and sugar bowls with blue gray; around the red triangles and the blue motifs in the border with yellow brown. Work all the remaining outline stitches in the border with dark gray blue. Frame the finished picture.

KEY TO CHART

		DMC	Anchor
·	= ecru (5 strands)	ecru	926
X	= dark rose (2 strands)	309	42
⊠	= green	368	214
◿	= light orange	402	336
✳	= gray	414	235
I	= light gray	415	234
△	= light brown	436	362
◣	= turquoise	518	168
(	= light turquoise	519	167
◢	= dark green	562	205
▲	= medium green	563	204
7	= yellow brown	676	874
∴	= light yellow	677	292
◠	= beige	738	942
◡	= flesh	739	885
O	= yellow	744	301
⌐	= old rose	760	36
—	= yellow green	772	259
/	= blue	799	145
)	= light blue	800	144
⟋	= pink	899	55
●	= dark gray blue (2 strands)	931	921
⟋	= light salmon	945	778
/	= light green	966	206
⋀	= moss green	989	257
\	= rose red	3328	10
\	= light pink	3716	25
⍀	= blue gray	3752	976
I	= light blue gray	3753	975
⊘	= dark salmon	3778	337

CHART FOR TREASURES FOR TEA TIME

A DAY AT THE BEACH

~

✂ Finished Measurements
25-1/2" x 20-3/4" (64 x 52 cm)

Materials
34" x 30" (85 x 75 cm) of cream Aida cloth with 11 threads per inch (2.5 cm); DMC embroidery floss as indicated on the chart; white and blue fabric paint; a flat brush; fabric fixative and a matching frame.

Directions
Wash and dry the Aida cloth and mark the finished measurements, using a washable marker or basting thread. Mix the two colors of paint to make two different shades: a light blue for the sky and a darker blue for the water. Paint the sky and water, let the fabric dry, and spray it with a fabric fixative.

Embroider the motifs in cross stitch by following the chart. Using one strand of floss, work each stitch over one thread. Embroider the eyes with three strands of black in French knots. Use one strand of gray floss for the tennis racket, weaving stitches over and under each other.

Using one strand of black floss, stem stitch the kite tail and line. Make three bows in dark blue, red, and pink, and attach them to the tail. Using three strands of floss, stem stitch around the darker kids with brown #632, under the sailboat on the right with black, and along the horizon with blue. Work the remaining stem stitches with a shade darker than the cross stitches to be outlined.

Frame the finished picture.

KEY TO CHART

		DMC
▼ =	black	310
△ =	gray	318
· =	white	white
● =	dark blue	797
◿ =	blue	826
⌄ =	light blue	806
L =	turquoise	996
◢ =	red brown	918
+ =	light red brown	922
⁒ =	sand	3064
○ =	light brown	3045
— =	yellow brown	3046
∷ =	beige	738
＼ =	yellow	973
⫽ =	green	702
V =	red	606
Z =	rose red	892
⌒ =	pink	760
	=	light pink	754
·. =	flesh color	951

NAPKINS WITH CHRISTMAS ROSES

✂ Finished Measurements
17-1/2" x 17-1/2" (44 x 44 cm)

Materials for 3 Napkins

18" (0.45 m) of white Flemish linen 64" (160 cm) wide with 28 threads per inch (2.5 cm); DMC or Anchor embroidery floss as indicated on the chart, plus dark red #498 or #47 and dark green #501 or #878; 12" (0.3 m) of red striped cotton 60" (150 cm) wide.

Directions

For each napkin, cut a square of linen 17-1/2" x 17-1/2" (44 x 44 cm). Cut two strips of striped cotton 1-1/2" x 17-1/2" (4 x 44 cm) and two strips 1-1/2" x 18-1/2" (4 x 46 cm). Sew the two short strips on opposite sides of the linen, with the right sides of linen and cotton together. Fold the cotton strip right side out along the stitching line, fold it over the edge of the linen, and slip stitch it to the other side, folding under the edge to make a smooth hem. Sew the two longer strips on opposite sides of the linen, making mitered corners

Embroider the motif in cross stitch, following the chart and beginning 1-1/4" (3 cm) from the striped border.

Using two strands of floss, work each cross stitch over two threads. Stem stitch around the flowers in dark red; work the veins in the leaves in dark green.

KEY TO CHART

		DMC	Anchor
☒	= red	347	13
⊞	= green	502	876
⊺	= light green	504	213
▷	= yellow	726	305
●	= shrimp	3328	10

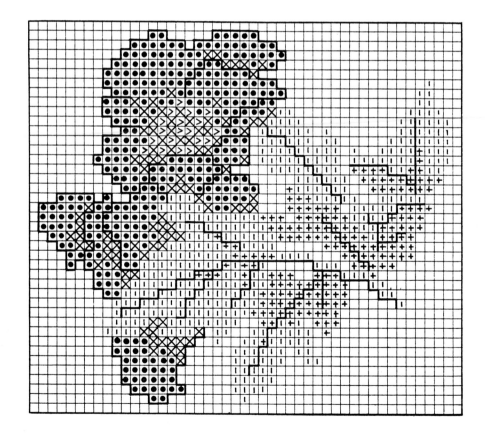

TEA COZY

✂ Finished Measurements
13-3/4" x 14-3/4" (35 x 37 cm)

KEY TO CHART 1: Tea Cozy

		DMC				DMC
□	= white	white	·	= beige	677
\	= dark red	304	\	= yellow	743
●	= black	310	O	= pale blue	775
–	= light blue	341	+	= dark blue	798
X	= dark gray	413	⊔	= light gray	928
⌐	= light brown	613	✳	= orange brown	977
/	= gray	647	v	= green	3012
θ	= red	666			

Materials

18" x 18" (45 x 45 cm) Aida cloth with 8 thread groups per inch (2.5 cm); DMC embroidery floss as indicated on the chart. For the back: 16" x 16" (40 x 40 cm) of gray-and-white striped cotton; 1-1/4" x 1-1/4" (3 x 3 cm) piece

of red cotton; black cotton yarn. For the lining: 7/8 yd (0.8 m) white cotton 36" (90 cm) wide; fiberfill batting; a small amount of fiberfill stuffing.

Directions

Embroider the cat on Aida cloth in cross stitch according to the chart. Using one strand of floss, work each cross stitch over one thread group. For the stem stitches, use three strands of black floss. The heart on the cat is worked in white. Begin at the lower right corner 1-1/2" (4 cm) from the edge. Embroider the red heart separately, following the chart.

Cut out the embroidered pieces, adding 1/2" (1.5 cm) seam allowance around all edges. Using these pieces as patterns, cut a back for each. Cut the cat from the gray striped fabric and the heart from red. For the cat, cut two pieces from the white cotton and two pieces of batting for lining. Trim 1/8" (3 mm) from the outer edges of the lining and batting pieces, but do not trim the lower edges.

Sew the embroidered cat to the striped backing with right sides together and 1/2" seam allowance, leaving the lower edge open. Trim the seams and turn right side out.

To make the lining, place a piece of batting on the wrong side of each piece of cotton and stitch around all edges with 1/4" (1 cm) seam allowance. With the cotton sides together, sew the two pieces with 1/2" seam allowance around the outer edges only, leaving the lower edge open. Trim seams close to the stitching and insert the lining in the cat. Turn the seam allowances at the lower edges to the inside and stitch together.

Sew the backing to the embroidered heart in the same way, leaving an opening. Trim seams, turn right side out, and stuff lightly with fiberfill. Stitch the opening. With black yarn, stitch the heart to the cat under the black bow.

EGG WARMERS

~

✂ Finished Measurements
3-1/2" x 3-1/2" (9 x 9 cm)

Materials

10" x 10" (25 x 25 cm) Aida cloth with 8 thread groups per inch (2.5 cm); DMC embroidery floss as indicated on Charts 2 and 3. For the lining: 10" x 10" cotton fabric.

Directions

Embroider the cats in cross stitch following the charts, working one strand over one thread group. Leave 1-1/4" (3 cm) between the embroidered areas. Cut out the embroidered pieces, adding 1/2" (1.5 cm) seam allowance around all edges. Use the embroidered pieces as patterns to cut two pieces of lining for each egg warmer.

Sew each embroidered front piece to a back with right sides together, leaving the lower edges open. Trim the seams and turn right side out. Construct the linings in the same way. Insert the linings in the cats. Turn the seam allowances at the lower edges to the inside and stitch together.

KEY TO CHART 2:
Egg Warmer, Black Cat

		DMC
·	= white	white
●	= dark red	304
◣	= black	310
✕	= gray	414
╱	= light gray	415
∷	= green	563
∅	= red	666

Work the whiskers in the gray and black sections in light gray. Work the remaining stem stitches in black.

KEY TO CHART 3:
Egg Warmer, Brown Cat

		DMC
·	= white	white
●	= dark red	304
■	= black	310
∷	= green	563
∅	= red	666
◣	= dark brown	918
╲	= brown	976
╱	= light brown	977
⌐	= yellow	3047

Work the stem stitches in black.

Black Cat

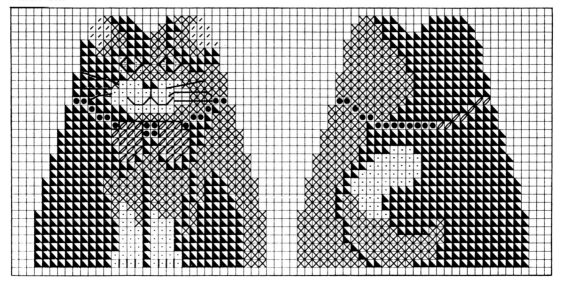

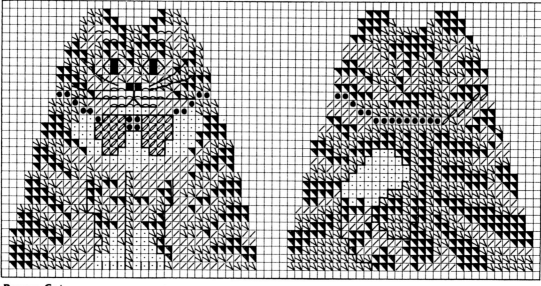

Brown Cat

PILLOW WITH BLUE CORNFLOWERS

~

✂ Finished Measurements
11" x 14" (28 x 35 cm)

Materials

12" (30 cm) of fine white linen 60" (150 cm) wide; 12" x 14" (30 x 35 cm) of even-weave linen with 30 threads per inch (2.5 cm); DMC embroidery floss in blue #796 or Anchor embroidery floss in blue #176; 2 yds (1.75 m) of white eyelet lace about 1-1/2" (4 cm) wide; a pillow form to fit.

Directions

Cut two pieces of fine linen 9-1/2" x 10-1/4" (24 x 26 cm) for the back. For the front, cut a piece 9-1/2" x 12" (24 x 30 cm).

With basting thread, mark a 9-1/2" x 12" rectangle in the center of the even-weave fabric. Embroider the flower motif in each of the four cor-

ners, placing each motif 1/2"
(1.5 cm) from the edges. Using
two strands of floss, work each
cross stitch over two threads. Draw
the stems and tendrils with a light
pencil, then embroider them in
stem stitch.

Along the long edges of both
back pieces, make a 1/4" (1 cm)
hem. Right sides up, overlap the
two back pieces so that, combined,
they make one piece 10-1/4" x 12-
3/4" (26 x 32 cm). Tack the short
edges temporarily. (Eventually, this
opening in the back will allow you

to insert and remove the pillow form.)
Sew the eyelet lace together end to
end, right sides together, and pin the
lace circle around the outside of the
embroidered piece, right sides
together. The edges of the pillow front
and the lace should be even and the
lace should be gathered evenly. Baste
the fine linen front to the embroidered
piece. Lay the back piece on the front,
right sides together, and sew around
edges with a 1/4" seam. Remove the
tacking on the back opening, turn the
pillow cover right side out, and insert
the pillow form.

KEY TO CHART		
	DMC	Anchor
● = blue	793	176

SHEET AND BIB WITH MICE

~

CRIB SHEET

✂ Finished Measurements
40" x 50" (100 x 125 cm)

✂ Border Measurements
2-1/2" (6.5 cm) wide

BIB

✂ Finished Measurements
6-1/4" x 7" (16 x 18 cm)

✂ Embroidery Measurements
2-1/4" x 4" (5.5 x 10 cm)

Directions for Crib Sheet

Materials

40" (1 m) of white Aida cloth 2-1/2" (6.5 cm) wide with 11 thread groups per inch (2.5 cm); DMC embroidery floss as indicated on the chart; 1-1/2 yds (1.25 m) of green striped cotton 40" wide.

Directions

Embroider the mice on the Aida cloth strip by following the chart, using two strands of floss and working each stitch over one thread group. Use one strand of gray for the stem stitches. Repeat the mice motif along the Aida cloth.

Make a 1" hem on all four sides of the striped cotton, turning under 1/4" (1 cm) of the outside edge for a neat double hem. Make a 1" hem on

each end of the Aida cloth strip. Adjust the fit, if necessary, then sew the strip to the sheet 2-1/4" (5.5 cm) from the top edge.

Directions for Bib

Materials

7" x 8" (18 x 20 cm) of white Aida cloth with 11 thread groups per inch (2.5 cm); 7" x 8" of white cotton; 1-1/4 yd (1.1 m) of light green bias tape; DMC embroidery floss as indicated on the chart.

Directions

Using the graph, make a paper pattern and use it to cut out the Aida cloth and the white cotton. Center the cross stitch chart on the Aida

cloth and begin work at point M, 1-1/4" (3.5 cm) from the lower edge. Using two strands of floss, work each stitch over one thread group. Use one strand of gray for stem stitches.

Place the white cotton and embroidered Aida cloth wrong sides together and baste around the edges. Sew one piece of bias seam binding around the bib, starting at one side of the bib and ending at the other side. Center a second piece of bias binding at the center of the neck and sew the two together, leaving 8" (20 cm) ties at each end.

KEY TO CHARTS

		DMC
⠿ = light gray		415
● = gray		317
V = green		955
— = pink		353
· = yellow		744

PATTERN FOR BIB

1 square = 1-1/2" (4 cm)

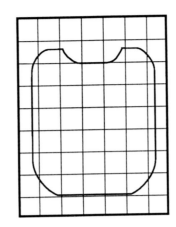

Motif for Crib Sheet

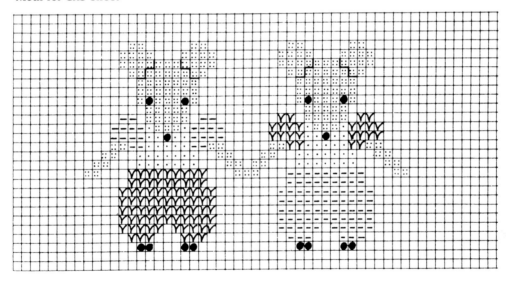

Motif for Bib

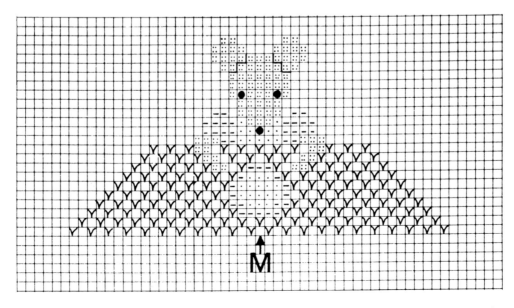

BED LINENS WITH BLUE FLOWERS

~

PILLOWCASES

✂ Border
2-1/2" (6 cm) wide

Materials

2 pillowcases; white Hardanger cloth with 25 double threads per inch (2.5 cm), about 2-1/2" wide and 1-3/4 yds (1.6 m) long; DMC embroidery floss as indicated on the chart.

Directions

Cut the Hardanger cloth in two equal pieces lengthwise. Embroider the border on both pieces, as on the towel. Hem the edges of the Hardanger cloth pieces and sew them to the pillowcases, 4" (10 cm) from the top.

TRAY CLOTH

✂ Finished Measurements
22-1/4" x 22-1/4" (56 x 56 cm)

✂ Border
2-3/4" (7 cm) wide

Materials

28" x 28" (70 x 70 cm) of white Hardanger fabric with 22 double threads per inch (2.5 cm); DMC embroidery floss as indicated on the chart.

Directions

Mark the horizontal and vertical centers of the fabric. Embroider the motif by following the chart. Make each cross stitch using three strands of floss over two double threads. Begin the embroidery at point M, 221 double threads from the center. Embroider the motif once to each corner. Embroider all four sides of the cloth (twice on each side). If desired, count eight double threads above and below the embroidered motif and make an openwork hem at both sides. For each ladder stitch, use one strand of light blue floss over two double threads. Make a 1" hem with a 1/4" (1 cm) inner hem and mitered corners.

TOWEL

✂ Border
2-1/2" (6 cm) wide

Materials

Blue-and-white striped towel; white Hardanger cloth with 25 double threads per inch (2.5 cm), about 2-1/2" (6 cm) wide and as long as the towel is wide plus 2" (5 cm); DMC embroidery floss as indicated on the chart.

Directions

Embroider the motif by following the chart. Make each cross stitch using three strands of floss over two double

threads. Begin embroidery at point A, centering the chart. Repeat the motif across the entire length of the Hardanger cloth. Hem the Hardanger cloth and sew it to the towel.

KEY TO CHART		
		DMC
X = green		702
+ = light green		704
● = dark blue		797
V = blue		799
— = light blue		800
O = yellow		973

CHART FOR PILLOWCASES, TRAY CLOTH, AND TOWELS

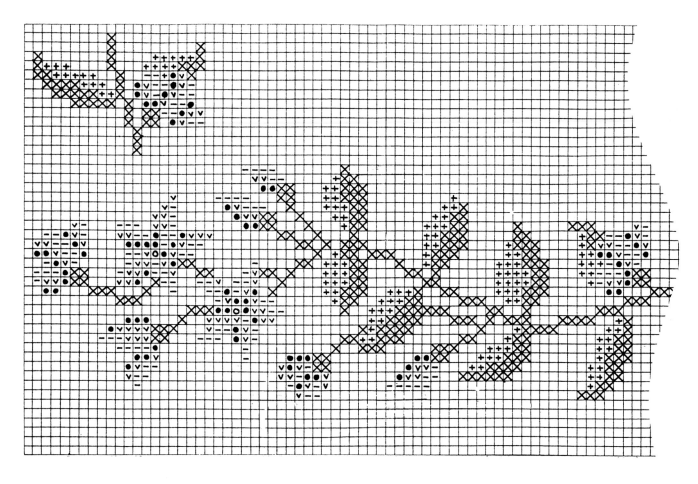

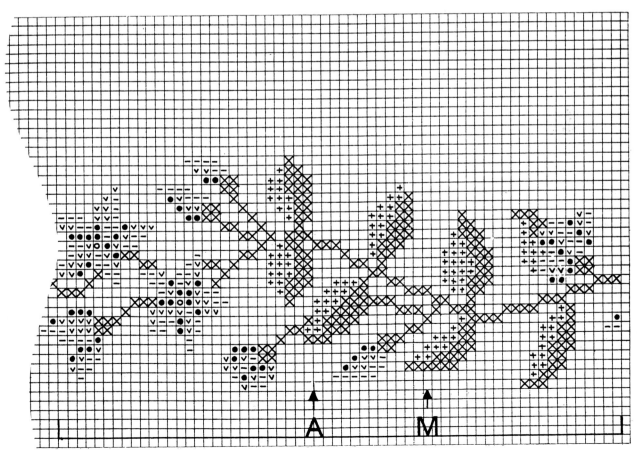

A M

NAPKIN WITH PEAR

~

✂ **Finished Measurements**
17" x 17" (43 x 43 cm)

Materials

White linen fabric about 18" x 18" (44.5 x 44.5 cm) with 30 threads per inch; DMC embroidery floss as indicated on the chart.

Directions

Mark a center square about 16" x 16" (41.5 x 41.5 cm) on the fabric. Embroider the blue border inside the square in cross stitch, using two strands of floss over two threads. Beginning three threads below the square, make a 1/8" (3 mm) openwork

hem with mitered corners, gathering three threads. In one corner, embroider the red pear motif, beginning the motif 1-1/4" (3 cm) from the side edge. Finish in stem stitch embroidery as shown in the photo.

	KEY TO CHART	
		DMC
\\	= sea green	504
\\	= blue	798
☐	= salmon	351
L	= old rose	760
\\	= light pink	818
X	= green	501
◠	= light green	502
\\	= pale green	503
Z	= olive green	3347
▼	= brown	433
H	= peach	402
Λ	= yellow	744
⌐	= camel	422

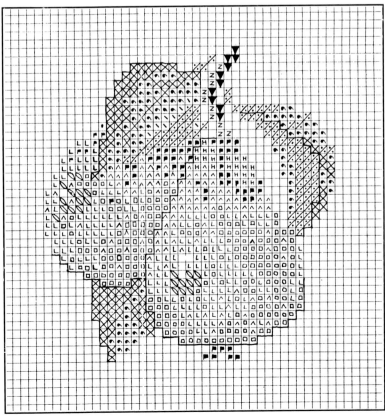

SHOPPING BAG

~

✂ Finished Measurements
20" x 22-3/4" (50 x 57 cm)

Materials

26" (.65 m) of ecru jute 56" (140 cm) wide with 12 threads per inch (2.5 cm); 24" (.6 m) of orange cotton 56" wide; DMC embroidery floss as indicated on the chart.

Directions

Mark a 20" x 24" (50 x 60 cm) rectangle on the jute. Embroider the motif on the jute, following the chart. Using one strand of floss, work each stitch over four threads. Begin at the lower right corner of the motif, 3-1/4" (8 cm) from the corner of the marked rectangle. Cut the jute 3/4" (2 cm) outside the marked rectangle. Cut a second piece the same size.

For the handles, cut two strips 3-1/4" x 22" (8 x 55 cm). For the lining, cut two pieces 21-1/2" x 23" (54 x 58 cm) from orange cotton. Place the jute pieces right sides together and sew along side and lower edge with 3/4" seam allowance. Fold in corners at lower edge and stitch in place over 4" (10 cm) to form a bottom to the bag. Make the lining in the same manner. Insert the lining in the bag, wrong sides together. The jute bag is 2-1/2" (6 cm) higher so you can make a 1-1/4" (3 cm) inner hem. Sew the hem in place.

Fold the handle strips in half, right sides together, and sew along narrow ends and along the side, leaving an opening to turn. Turn right side out and sew opening closed. Topstitch along all edges. Sew the handles to the bag as shown in the photo, 5-3/4" (14.5 cm) from the side seams and 1-1/4" from the sides.

KEY TO CHART

		DMC
L	= ecru	ecru
Z	= brown	2840
\	= yellow	2743
O	= orange	2923
X	= blue	2797
::	= bright green	2369
·	= light green	2472
—	= green	2471
/	= dark green	2986
v	= hunter green	2909
II	= light hunter green	2911
H	= brown green	2392
I	= gray green	2320

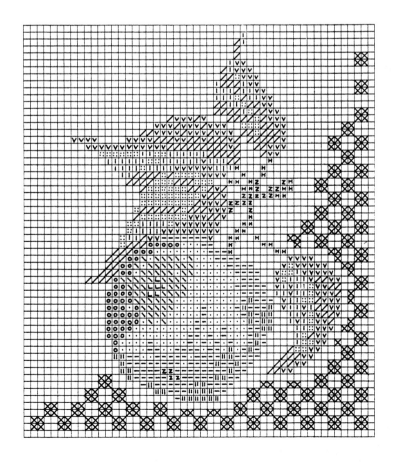

73

CHRISTMAS ORNAMENTS

~

Materials

For each ornament: a piece of linen with 25 threads per inch (2.5 cm). For the Santa and the bear, 6" x 8" (15 x 20 cm) piece of linen; for each of the remaining motifs, a 6" x 6" (15 x 15 cm) piece of linen. DMC embroidery floss as indicated on the chart; fiberfill batting for the stuffing; a piece of cotton in matching colors for the back.

Directions

Embroider the motifs in cross stitch by following the chart. Place each motif in the center of a piece of linen. Using three strands of floss, work each cross stitch over two threads. Use two strands of black floss for the stem stitches.

Pin the piece of cotton to the embroidered linen, right sides together, and pin the batting to the wrong side of the linen. Sew around the edges with 1/4" (1 cm) seam allowance, leaving an opening through which to turn the ornament right side out. Trim the edges, turn, and sew the opening closed. Sew a loop of red floss to the top, as a hanger.

KEY TO CHART

Symbol	Color	DMC		Symbol	Color	DMC
·	= white	white		0	= green	702
I	= yellow	307		⅄	= light green	704
◢	= black	310		ᴗ	= beige	738
∧	= orange brown	402		◠	= light beige	739
⊥	= gray	414		∴	= light flesh	754
☐	= light gray	415		o	= flesh	761
◨	= soft brown	436		◥	= dark blue	796
╲	= pale brown	437		◿	= blue	798
⋀	= dark red	498		✳	= wine red	814
◤	= very dark green	500		I	= dark orange brown	922
╱	= pink	603		)	= light pink	957
X	= red	666		/	= dark yellow	973
∕	= yellow brown	676		⋰	= turquoise	996
◸	= gold brown	680		◹	= brown	3045
●	= dark green	700				

BOX WITH VIOLETS

✂ Embroidery Measurements
6" x 12" (15 x 30 cm)

Materials

24" (0.6 m) of light blue Hardanger cloth 60" (150 cm) wide with 22 threads per inch (2.5 cm); purchased box about 13-1/4" x 17-1/4" (33 x 43.5 cm); DMC or Anchor embroidery floss as indicated on the chart; white craft glue.

Directions

Cut a 20" x 24" (50 x 60 cm) piece of Hardanger cloth and embroider it by following the chart. Begin at the lower right corner at point A, 6" (15 cm) from the right edge. Using two strands of floss, work each cross stitch over two double threads.

Using one strand of floss, stem stitch around the periwinkle violets with dark blue. Work the remaining stem stitches in black.

For the 10-3/4" x 15" (27 x 38 cm) border, begin 36 double threads from the right edge and 29 double threads from the left edge; and 27 double threads from the lower edge and 27 double threads from the top cross stitch. Run a basting thread along these measurements. Run a second thread eight double threads inside the first basting thread. Cross stitch the bow at the center of the top border. Using two strands, work each stitch over two double threads. Embroider the stem stitches with two strands of floss. Now work the border in satin stitch, using one strand of medium blue. Center the fabric on top of the box and glue the fabric to the box, mitering the corners on the inside of the lid.

KEY TO CHARTS

		DMC	Anchor
·	= white	white	1
)	= azalea	3609	96
\	= pale plum	554	98
0	= dark lilac	553	100
◣	= light plum	208	102
◊	= purple	550	111
◡	= pale blue lilac	341	117
7	= periwinkle	340	118
\	= very pale blue	775	128
▲	= dark blue	798	132
/	= light blue	800	144
:	= medium blue	809	145

		DMC	Anchor
✳	= blue	797	146
●	= dark moss green	319	218
/	= light green	966	241
\	= green	703	243
✕	= medium green	702	245
—	= light moss green	702	264
⧄	= moss green	3348	266
○	= yellow	444	297
■	= black	310	403
⌐	= gray	3072	900
\	= dark green	699	923

CHARTS FOR BOX WITH VIOLETS

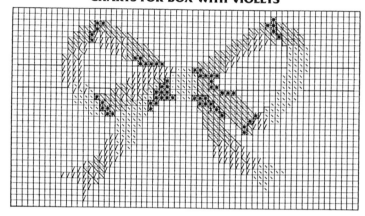

Delft Blue Bath Set

~

Rug

✂ Finished Measurements
24-3/4" x 36" (62 x 90 cm)

Materials

1 yd (.75 m) white double-thread rug canvas 40" (100 cm) wide with 18 squares per four inches (10 cm); Mayflower Helarsgarn in indicated colors and Mayflower Cotton 8 dark blue #527; 3.5 yds (3.15 m) twill tape 2" (5 cm) wide.

Directions

Tape the edges of the canvas to keep it from unravelling while you work on it. Begin embroidery at lower right corner 3-1/4" (8 cm) from the edge. Embroider by following the chart. Use one strand of Helarsgarn over one double canvas thread. When the center motif is complete, embroider the border. Working from inside out, work one row of white, three rows of blue and three rows of medium blue. Work stem stitches using two strands of dark blue #527. Trim around 1-1/4" (3 cm) from outside of embroidery and fold to wrong side. Sew twill tape around the rug to cover the edges.

CHART FOR WASHCLOTH

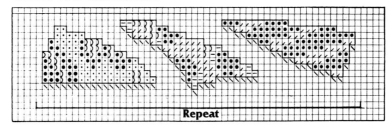

CHART FOR TOWEL

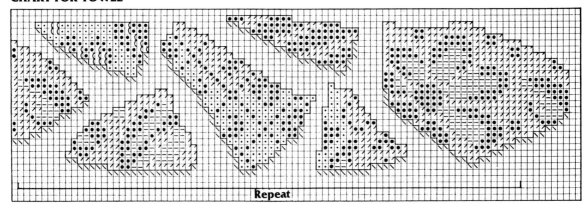

CHART FOR RUG

KEY TO CHART FOR RUG

		Mayflower
☐	= white	902
●	= blue	906
−	= medium blue	919
·	= light blue	958
╲	= light green	1011
I	= lilac	1021

KEY TO CHARTS FOR WASH CLOTH & HAND TOWEL

		DMC	Anchor
╱	= white	white	1
╲	= lilac	210	108
·	= light green	747	158
●	= dark blue	796	134
−	= blue	799	145
⊃	= light blue	800	144

Wash Cloth

✂ Embroidered Band
1-1/4" (3 cm) wide

Materials

White wash cloth; 16" (40 cm) white Hardanger cloth band 1-1/4" (3 cm) wide with 25 double threads per inch (2.5 cm); DMC or Anchor embroidery floss as indicated on the chart; braided cord.

Directions

Embroider the Hardanger cloth band in cross stitch, centering the chart. Using two strands of floss, work each cross stitch over two double threads. Begin 1-1/2" (4 cm) from right edge (a narrow edge). Repeat the motif across the band for the width of the towel. Work stem stitches in dark blue #823 or #150. Cut the band 1/2"(1.5 cm) wider than the towel. Fold 1/4" (1 cm) at each end and sew to towel 1/4" from each side seam. Fold wrong sides together and sew along side and lower edge. Turn. Sew on braided cord in a loop.

Hand Towel

✂ Embroidered Band
2-1/2" (6 cm) wide

Materials

White hand towel 20" (50 cm) wide; 24" (60 cm) strip of white Hardanger cloth 2-1/2" (6 cm) wide with 25 double threads per inch (2.5 cm); DMC or Anchor embroidery floss as indicated on the chart.

Directions

Work the Hardanger cloth band in cross stitch by following the chart. Using two strands of floss, work each stitch over two double threads. Begin 1-1/2" (4 cm) from the right edge (a narrow edge). Repeat the motif for the width of the towel. Work the stem stitches in dark blue #823 or #150. Cut the band 1/2" (1.5 cm) wider than the towel, fold under 1/4" (1 cm) at each end, and sew to towel.

81

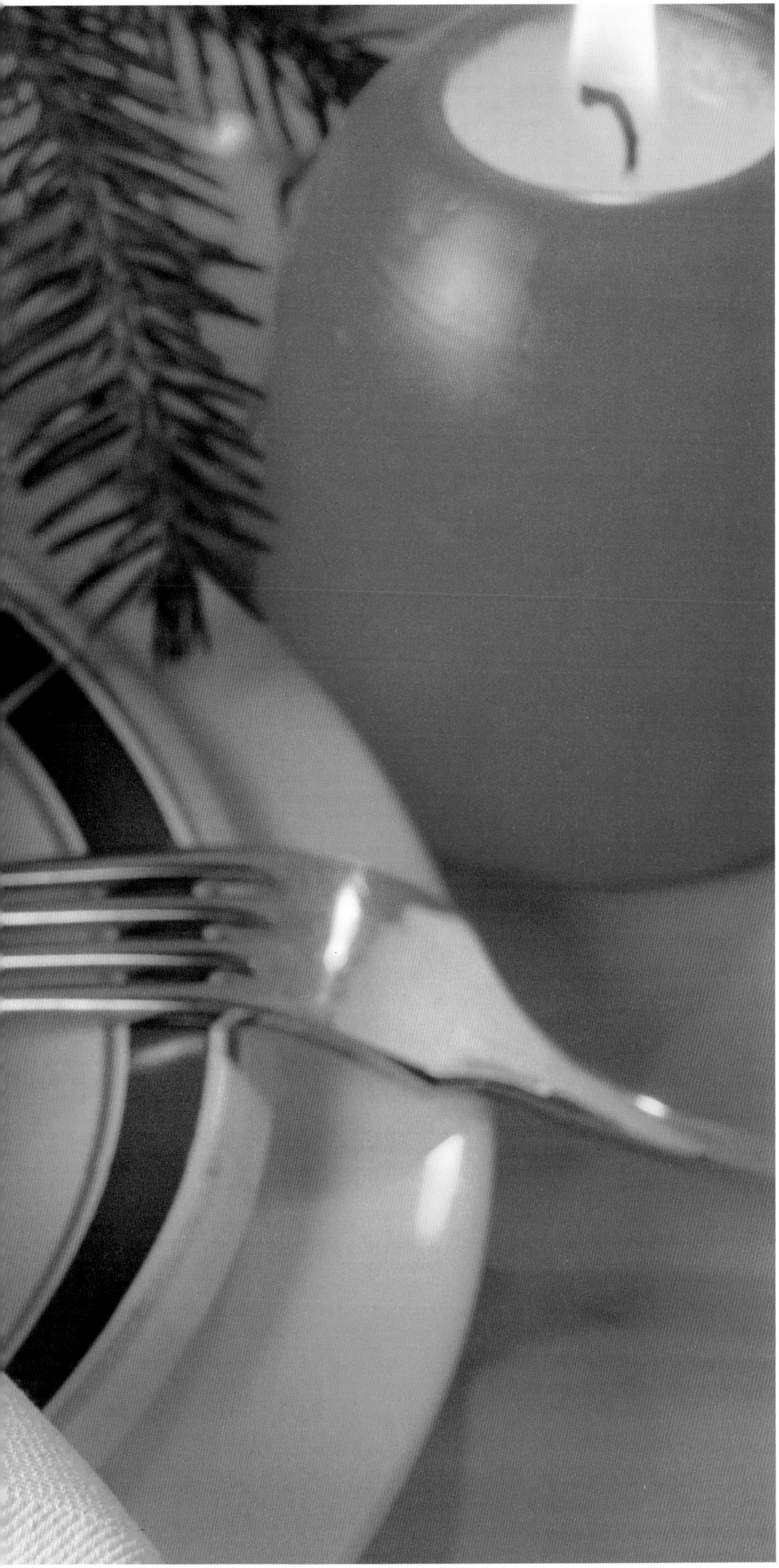

NAPKIN RING WITH HOLLY

✂ Finished Measurements
1-3/4" (4.5 cm) wide

Materials
7" (18 cm) length of white Aida band 1-3/4" (4.5 cm) wide, with a red edge (optional) and 14 thread groups per inch (2.5 cm); DMC or Anchor embroidery floss as indicated on the chart; white sewing thread.

Directions
Embroider the motif by centering the chart on the Aida band. Using two strands of floss, work each stitch over one thread group. Sew the narrow ends together, right sides together, with a 1/4" (1 cm) seam.

KEY TO CHART

	DMC	Anchor
✳ = dark red	304	799
■ = black	310	403
▽ = gray green	562	221
/ = light gray green	563	204
⧅ = red	666	46
● = dark green	699	923
✕ = green	702	226
— = pink	956	40
◡ = yellow green	3348	264

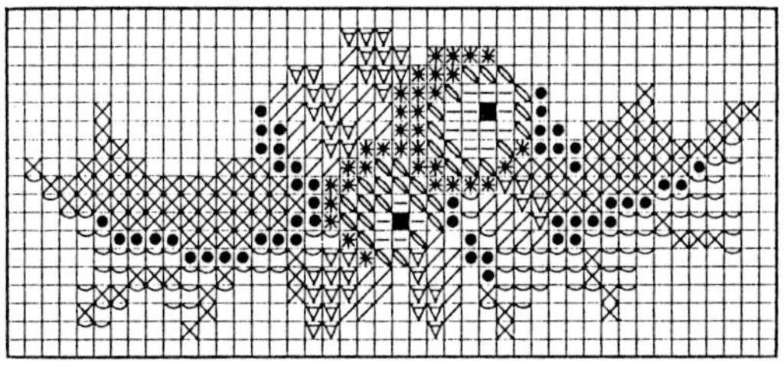

CURTAINS WITH JONQUILS

✂ Finished Measurements
6" x 16" (15 x 40 cm)

Materials

White linen with 25 threads per inch (2.5 cm). (Measure the length and width of area to be covered; allow twice the width and 16-3/4" (42 cm) extra in length for upper and lower

84

hems.) Embroidery cotton in colors indicated on the chart, plus light brown and white floss; pleater tape or curtain rings.

Directions

Mark the desired length on the fabric. Make 1/2" (1.5 cm) side hems, turn under 1/4" (1 cm) of the edge to form an inner hem. Make a 4-3/4" (12 cm) hem at the lower edge with an inner hem the same width. Ten threads above the hem, make an openwork hem. Use staggered ladder stitch, working each stitch over eight threads and using three strands of white floss.

Embroider the motif in cross stitch,

following the chart. Using one strand of embroidery cotton, work each stitch over four threads. Repeat the motif along the entire width of the curtain above the openwork hem, as shown in the photo.

Stem stitch in and around the flowers with light brown and orange; work the remaining stem stitches in the color of the neighboring cross stitch or one shade darker.

Make a 3-1/2" (9 cm) hem at the top with an inner hem the same width. Pleat the top of the curtain by using pleater tape (follow the package directions) or by making individual drapery pleats.

KEY TO CHART

⌒ =	light green
T =	green
● =	dark green
⊠ =	light yellow green
✕ =	yellow green
◣ =	blue green
◠ =	orange
◩ =	light orange
Λ =	yellow
(=	pale yellow
⟋ =	pale brown
○ =	brown
Λ̸ =	dark brown
◢ =	very dark brown
· =	white

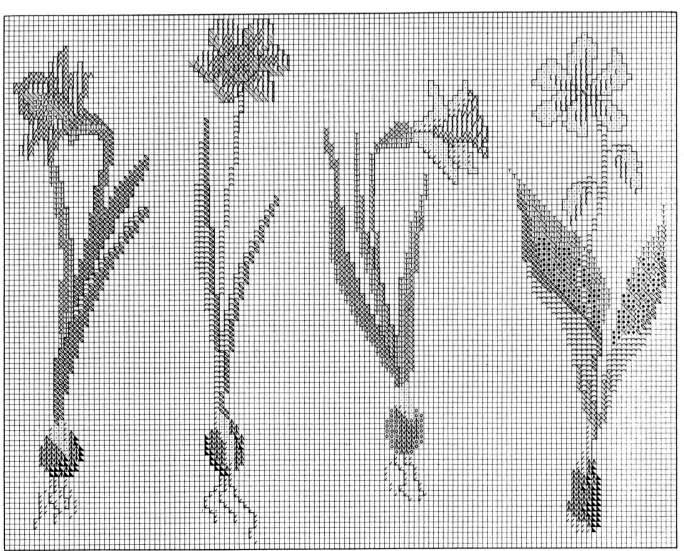

BATH LINENS WITH BERRIES

~

✂ Width of Embroidered Band
2-1/2" (6 cm)

Materials
Two pink or white Hardanger bands 2-1/2" (6 cm) wide with 22 double threads per inch (2.5 cm): one should be 1" longer than the width of the towel, the other 1" longer than the width of the wash cloth; DMC embroidery floss as indicated on the chart; pink or white towel and washcloth.

Directions
Embroider the motif in cross stitch on the Hardanger band.

Using two strands of floss, work each stitch over two double threads, beginning at the lower right edge and working across. Hem the narrow ends of the band and sew it to the towel 4" (10 cm) from the lower edge, using small stitches and two strands of pink or white floss. Work each stitch over two double threads and place stitches two double threads apart. See photo.

Follow the same procedure for the washcloth but work the flowers in white.

<table>
<tr><td colspan="3">KEY TO CHART</td></tr>
<tr><td></td><td></td><td>DMC</td></tr>
<tr><td>●</td><td>= white or rose</td><td>335</td></tr>
<tr><td>X</td><td>= green</td><td>989</td></tr>
</table>

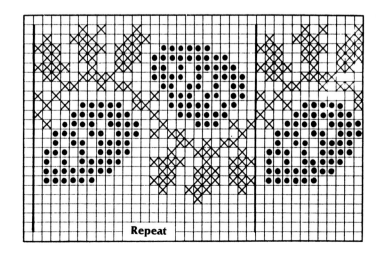

Repeat

CURTAINS WITH GERANIUMS

～

✂ Finished Measurements
24" x 32" (60 x 80 cm)

✂ Embroidery Measurements
7" x 9-1/4" (17.5 x 23.5 cm)

Materials
28" (0.7 m) of white linen 56" (140 cm) wide with 35 threads per inch (2.5 cm); DMC embroidery floss as indicated on the chart.

Directions
Cut one piece of linen 28" x 36" (70 x 90 cm) and one piece 10-1/4" x 28" (26 x 70 cm). On the large piece, embroider a geranium in cross stitch, centering the chart. Using three strands of floss, work each stitch over seven threads. Begin the geranium at center 4-1/4" (11 cm) from lower edge. Embroider a geranium on each side of the center one, spaced 168 threads away, measured from the bottom of the pot.

Embroider the border in cross stitch, following the chart. Place the border 17 threads from the lower edge of the pot and begin 74 threads from the outside cross stitch of the pot. Make each cross stitch with three strands of rose floss over seven threads. Repeat the chart six times.

Cut the embroidered linen in a rectangle 25-1/2" x 33-1/2" (64 x 84 cm), with the lower edge 2-1/2" (6 cm) below the border and the side seam 1" (2.5 cm) from the beginning of the border.

Embroider the small piece with a border placed 2-1/2" from the lower edge and 1-1/4" (3 cm) from the right edge. Cut a linen rectangle 10-1/4" x 25-1/2" (26 x 64 cm). Make a 1" hem at the lower edge with an inner hem. Hem the sides with a 1/4" (1 cm) hem and an inner hem. At the top, make a 1/4" inner hem and an outer hem 2" (5 cm) wide. Stitch in place at top.

Border Chart

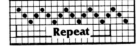

Repeat

KEY TO CHART

		DMC
─	= green	701
●	= rose red	891
╱	= dark brown	920
✕	= brown	921

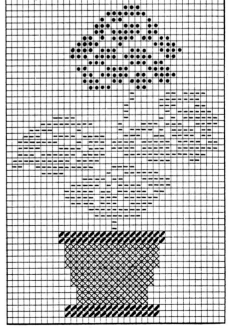

89

PILLOW WITH GERANIUMS

~

✂ Finished Measurements
18" x 18" (45 x 45 cm)

✂ Embroidery Measurements
10" x 10" (25 x 25 cm)

Materials
16" x 16" (40 x 40 cm) of white Aida
cloth with 10 thread groups per inch
(2.5 cm); DMC embroidery floss as
indicated on the chart, plus dark gray
#317 and gray blue #931; 14" x 20"
(35 x 50 cm) of blue-and-white-

striped cotton; two pieces of cotton
14" x 20"; zipper 14" (35 cm) long;
pillow form to fit.

Directions
Embroider the Aida cloth in cross
stitch, following the chart. Begin at
the lower right corner at point A, 2-
3/4" (7 cm) from the lower edge and
6-3/4" (17 cm) from the right edge.
Using three strands of floss, work each
cross stitch over one thread group.
Note: In some cases you will use two
or three colors of floss together to
form a new color.

Cut the Aida cloth 19 thread
groups from the outside of the motif.
Cut out four strips of striped cotton 3-
1/4" x 20" (8 x 50 cm) and sew them
to the four edges of the Aida cloth,
right sides together, using 1/4" (1 cm)

seam allowances and making mitered
corners. Sew the two pieces of cotton
together along two long edges (the
center back seam), leaving an opening
14" (35 cm) long, and sew in the zipper. Place the back and front pieces
right sides together, and pin. Insert
the pillow form and sew around three
sides. Open the zipper and sew up
the fourth side. Remove the form, turn
the pillowcase right side out, and re-
insert the form.

Using two strands of floss, stem
stitch around the vase and around the
pink and white geraniums in gray blue
#931. Stem stitch around the rose gera-
nium in dark red; around the red geranium in dark gray #317; around the
leaves in bright green. Work the blue
spots in dark blue and the other colors
as indicated on the chart.

KEY TO CHART

		DMC				DMC				DMC
·	= white	white	▼	= dark sea green	500	=	= light blue gray	927
⏐	= ecru	ecru (1),	+	= gray green	524	∅	= pink	961
		504 (1),	△	= grass green	702	Z	= dark green	991
		white (1)	∧	= old rose	778	O	= mint green	993
∕	= red	304	＼	= dark blue	792	✎	= dark moss green	3011
N	= gray	318	X	= blue	793	·	= pale gray	white (2),
⁄	= yellow green	445 (2),	□	= light blue	800			3072 (1)
		472 (1)	●	= rose red	892	─	= light moss green	3348
⌐	= green	471	V	= light grass green	906	■	= dark red	3685
＼	= light green	472	∥	= blue gray	793 (1),			
					926 (2)			

TABLECLOTH WITH BLUE FLOWERS

✂ Finished Measurements
44" x 56" (110 x 140 cm)

Materials
1-1/2 yds (1.3 m) of white linen 64" (160 cm) wide with 28 threads per inch (2.5 cm); DMC embroidery floss as indicated on the chart, plus dark blue #823; white sewing thread.

Directions
Mark the horizontal and vertical centers of the cloth. Place the large center motif at the center of the cloth with the lower edge of the motif parallel to a long side of the cloth. (The two M's should read correctly when parallel to a long side.) Using two strands of floss, work each cross stitch over three threads. Using three strands of floss, stem stitch along the flowers in dark blue #823 and along the green sections in hunter green. Embroider the small motifs scattered around the tablecloth, using the photo as a guide and working all motifs at least 7-1/2" (19 cm) from the outside edges.

Embroider the border motif in cross stitch, following the chart and placing the corner 6" (15 cm) from the edge. Repeat the motif to next corner, and work the motif around the cloth. Work the repeats 10 times along the short sides and 14 times along the long sides. Using two strands of floss, work each cross stitch over three threads.

Trim the cloth to 5-1/4" (13 cm) from the lower edge of the lower border. Make a hem 1-1/2" (4 cm) wide with a 1/4" (1 cm) inner hem and mitered corners. Three threads above the top of the hem and 2" (5 cm) from each edge, make an openwork hem using white sewing thread, gathering four threads in each stitch.

KEY TO CHART

		DMC
—	= green	702
●	= blue	798
⌐	= turquoise	519
+	= brown gray	645
I	= yellow	3078
∅	= hunter green	890
II	= spruce	561
L	= seafoam	504
∩	= moss green	3348
(	= light blue	827

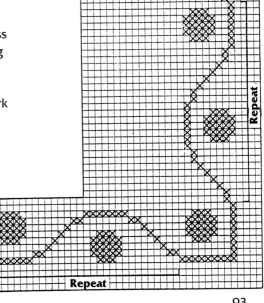

CHART FOR BORDER MOTIF

Repeat

Repeat

MOTIF FOR TABLECLOTH WITH BLUE FLOWERS

TOWEL WITH SEALS

~

✂ Finished Measurements
of Embroidery
1-3/4" (4.5 cm) wide

Materials
A red-and-white striped towel 22" (55 cm) wide; 24" (60 cm) length of white Aida band 1-3/4" wide, with a red edge (optional) and 19 threads per inch (2.5 cm); DMC embroidery floss as indicated on the chart.

Directions
Embroider the seals in cross stitch, following the chart and using two strands of floss over one thread. Place the first seal 2" (5 cm) from the right edge, then embroider six seals across, spaced 12 strands apart. For stem stitch outlines, use one strand of black floss. Hem the edges of the band and sew it to the towel.

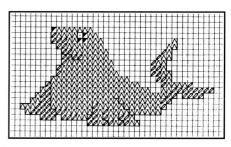

KEY TO CHART

		DMC
·	= white	white
◣	= black	310
0	= medium gray	647
V	= light gray	648

TABLE LINENS WITH PINK LILIES

~

NAPKIN

✂ Finished Measurements
14" x 14" (35 x 35 cm)

Materials
For each napkin, 16" x 16" (40 x 40 cm) of white linen with 25 threads per inch (2.5 cm); DMC embroidery floss as indicated on the chart, plus light blue #828.

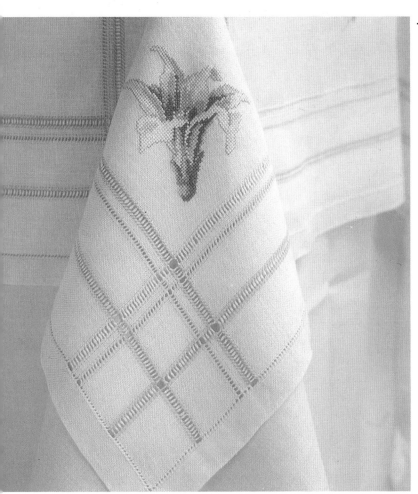

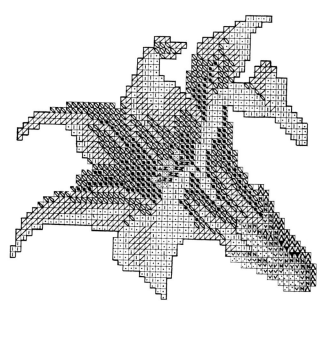

Directions

Make a 1-1/4" (3 cm) hem with a 1/4" (1 cm) inner hem and mitered corners. Make an openwork hem and openwork borders with ladder stitch. Embroider lilies as on the tablecloth, placing one 1-1/2" from the openwork (see the photo).

TABLECLOTH

✂ Finished Measurements
52" x 64" (130 x 160 cm)

✂ Lily
4" x 4-1/4" (10 x 11 cm)

Materials

68" (1.7 m) of white linen 56" (140 cm) wide with 25 threads per inch (2.5 cm); DMC embroidery floss as indicated on the chart, plus light blue #828; tracing paper and pencil.

Directions

Make a 1" hem with a 1/4" (1 cm) inner hem and mitered corners. Make an openwork hem, working ladder stitch two threads above the hem, beginning and ending 1-1/2" (4 cm) from the corners of the tablecloth. Work each ladder stitch over three threads, using two strands of light pink floss. Now work openwork borders on the tablecloth in ladder stitch. Place these borders 2", 3-1/2", 4", 13-1/2", and 14" (5, 9, 10.5, 34 and 35.5 cm) above the hem. Work the borders over varying numbers of threads, as shown in the photo. At each side of border, work in ladder stitch. Use colored floss as you desire or use the photo as a guide.

Embroider single lilies in cross stitch scattered over the tablecloth. Trace the motif on tracing paper and pin it to the tablecloth. Using two strands of floss, work each stitch over two threads. Use one strand of pink

floss to stem stitch around the petals and one strand of green floss on the stem stitches in the rest of the motif.

KEY TO CHART		
		DMC
∧ = green		320
N = dark green		367
V = medium green		368
∴ = light green		369
Z = dark yellow		725
∷ = yellow		745
· = light yellow		746
△ = ochre		783
I = pale pink		819
/ = light pink		963
● = mauve		3350
⍀ = light mauve		3354

Christmas Tree Skirt

✂ Finished Measurements
34" x 34-1/2" (85 x 86 cm)

Materials
38-3/4" x 39" (97 x 98 cm)
of white Aida cloth with
lurex threads, about 8 thread
groups per inch (2.5 cm);
DMC embroidery floss as
indicated on the chart.

Directions

Mark the center of each side and embroider the Santa Claus and sleigh at the center, following the chart. Using one strand of floss, work each stitch over one thread group. Begin the motif 5" (12.5 cm) from the edge. On each corner, embroider the two small Christmas trees 5" from the edge and 57 threads from the corner. Between the small trees and the sleigh, embroider one large tree. Embroider a row of red cross stitches 3-1/2" (9 cm) from the edges. Using three strands of floss, stem stitch the Christmas bells with burgundy. Work the remaining stem stitches in black. Make a 1-1/4" (3 cm) hem with an inner hem and mitered corners.

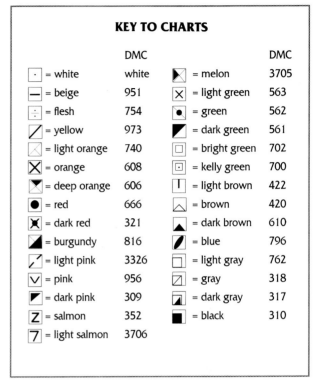

KEY TO CHARTS

		DMC			DMC
·	= white	white	◣	= melon	3705
—	= beige	951	☒	= light green	563
∷	= flesh	754	◉	= green	562
╱	= yellow	973	◢	= dark green	561
⊠	= light orange	740	□	= bright green	702
✕	= orange	608	⊡	= kelly green	700
▼	= deep orange	606	I	= light brown	422
●	= red	666	◺	= brown	420
�҉	= dark red	321	▲	= dark brown	610
◢	= burgundy	816	◿	= blue	796
◿	= light pink	3326	◻	= light gray	762
∨	= pink	956	◿	= gray	318
◤	= dark pink	309	◸	= dark gray	317
Z	= salmon	352	■	= black	310
7	= light salmon	3706			

PILLOW WITH VINING FLOWERS

✂ Finished Measurements
14-1/4" x 14-1/4"   (36 x 36 cm)

Materials

18" x 56" (.45 m x 140 cm) of white linen with 25 threads per inch (2.5 cm); DMC embroidery floss as indicated on the chart, plus dark salmon #350 and bright green #669; 12" (30 cm) zipper; pillow form.

Directions

Cut a square of linen 18" x 18" (45 x

45 cm) and two pieces 8-1/4" x 16" (21 x 40 cm). Mark the horizontal and vertical lines. Embroider the motifs in cross stitch, following the chart and centering at point M. Using two strands of floss, work each cross stitch over two threads. For the stem stitches, use two strands of floss; embroider around the leaves in bright green and around the flowers in dark salmon. Work the chart four times, once in each quadrant, to form a floral border around the pillow. Cross stitch a border 16 threads outside the flower motif. Work each cross stitch over two

threads, using three strands of dark salmon spaced two threads apart.

Trim the fabric to 1-1/4" (3 cm) outside the square. Place the two smaller pieces right sides together, and sew along one long side with a 1/2" (1.5 cm) seam allowance, leaving the center 12" (30 cm) open. Sew the zipper into the opening. Place the back piece right sides together with the embroidered top, and sew around the edges with a 1/4" (1 cm) seam allowance. Turn the pillowcase right side out and insert the pillow form.

KEY TO CHART

		DMC
·	= white	white
∧	= salmon	352
/	= yellow	445
⌐	= bright green	704
⌐	= light salmon	761
–	= light rose	819
●	= dark green	991
X	= green	992
/.	= light green	993

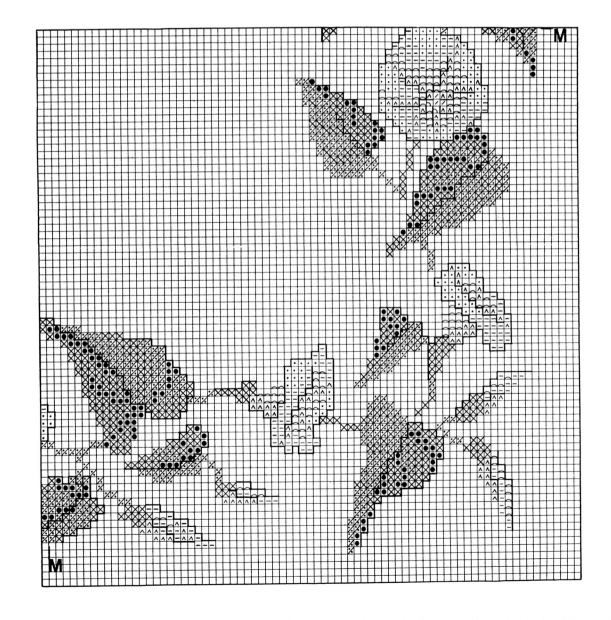

TABLE LINENS WITH LEMONS & TOMATOES

~

NAPKINS

✂ Finished Measurements
14-1/4" x 14-1/4" (36 x 36 cm)

✂ Border Motif
4" x 4" (10 x 10 cm)

Materials

16" x 16" (40 x 40 cm) of white Hardanger fabric with 22 double threads per inch (2.5 cm); DMC embroidery floss as indicated on the chart.

Directions

Mark the hemline 1/4" (1 cm) from each edge with inner hem. Make an openwork hem as on the tablecloth. Begin embroidery at the lower right corner, beginning on the first thread above the openwork. Work each cross stitch using two or three strands of floss, as on the tablecloth. Use two strands of floss for each stem stitch.

Motifs for Napkins

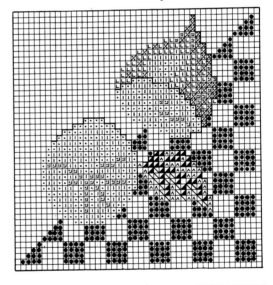

KEY TO CHARTS

		DMC
I	= bright yellow	307
L	= yellow	444
◢	= gray green	562
◠	= light gray green	563
⌐	= red	606
▲	= bright orange	608
◪	= grass green	702
◪	= light grass green	704
·	= yellow brown	734
∴	= orange	741
—	= pale gray	762
●	= blue	799
✕	= dark green	909
Λ	= green	913
＼	= pale green	955
／	= light green	966
·	= light yellow	3078
+	= medium orange	3340
＼	= light moss green	3348

103

TABLECLOTH

✂ Finished Measurements
62" x 62" (155 x 155 cm)

Materials
2 yds (1.65 m) of white Hardanger fabric 68" (170 cm) wide with 22 double threads per inch (2.5 cm); DMC embroidery floss as indicated on the chart.

Directions
Cut a square of Hardanger cloth 66" x 66" (165 x 165 cm). Mark the horizontal and vertical centers. Embroider the motif in cross stitch, centering point M at the center of the fabric. Work the motif four times around the fabric. Work each stitch over two double threads. For the tomatoes, the whole lemon, and the peel of the half lemon, use three strands of floss. For the slice and the interior of the half lemon, use two strands. For the light yellow stitches, use three strands. Embroider the remaining cross stitches with three strands.

Using two strands of floss, stem stitch along the tomatoes with dark red #817 and along the lemon with dark moss green #367. Work the edges in blue and the other stem stitches in dark green #909.

Make a 1" (2.5 cm) hem with an inner hem and mitered corners. If desired, work an openwork hem one double thread above the hem, forming right angles of openwork in each corner 1-1/4" (4 cm) from the edges. Work each openwork stitch over two double threads.

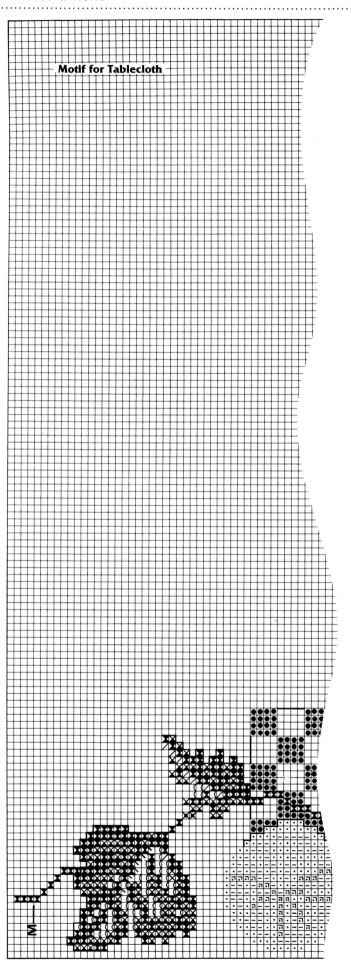

Motif for Tablecloth

~ CLOTHING & ACCESSORIES

GIRL'S JUMPER

~

Materials

Mother and Baby Ducks: 2-1/2" x 10" (6 x 25 cm) piece of linen with 20 threads per inch (2.5 cm). Row of Ducks: 2-1/2" x 8" (6 x 20 cm) piece of linen with 20 threads per inch (2.5 cm); DMC embroidery floss as indicated on the chart; purchased dress or jumper.

Directions

Mother and Baby Ducks: Cut a piece of linen 2" x 2-1/2" (5 x 6 cm) for the pocket embroidery. Pin the rest of the linen on the right side of the bodice of the dress. Embroider the ducks by following the chart, using three strands of floss over two threads. Embroider the mother duck first. Begin at point A, 3-1/2" (9 cm) from the left edge and 1" from the lower edge of front. Embroider six or seven ducklings. Trim the unembroidered linen away. Pin the 2" x 2-1/2" piece of linen on the pocket at center and embroider a duckling on the pocket as you did on the bodice.

Row of Ducks: Pin the linen to the right side of the dress bodice. Work the motif by following the chart, centering one duck at M. Begin 1/2" (1.5 cm) from the lower edge. Cross stitch five ducks, using two strands of floss over two threads.

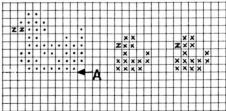

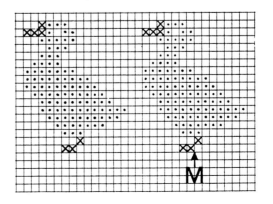

KEY TO CHARTS

		DMC
· = white		white
X = yellow		307
Z = orange		972

JACKET WITH TULIPS

~

Materials

White jacket made of linen or other even-weave fabric with 25 to 28 threads per inch (2.5 cm), or pieces of even-weave fabric large enough for the motifs; DMC embroidery floss as indicated on the chart.

Directions

Using two strands of floss, work each cross stitch over two threads. Work the large tulip on the right front of the jacket, beginning at point A, 1-1/4" (3.5 cm) from center front and 10" (25 cm) from lower edge. Embroider the second tulip beginning at point B, 8-1/2" (21.5 cm) from the lower edge and 4" (10 cm) from the center front. Begin the third tulip 6" (15.5 cm) from the center front and 10-1/4" (26 cm) from the lower edge.

Embroider the center tulip at the center edge on the left front of the jacket, beginning at point B, 1-1/2" (4 cm) from the center edge and 9-1/4" (23.5 cm) from the lower edge. Stem stitch around the leaves with grass green #702. Work the remaining stem stitches in colors to match the neighboring cross stitches or in one shade darker.

If a linen garment is unavailable, pin pieces of linen fabric to the garment and embroider through all thicknesses. Unravel the unembroidered fabric and trim the excess.

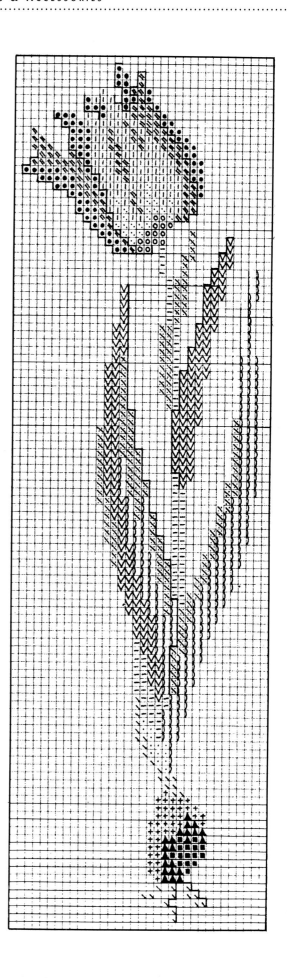

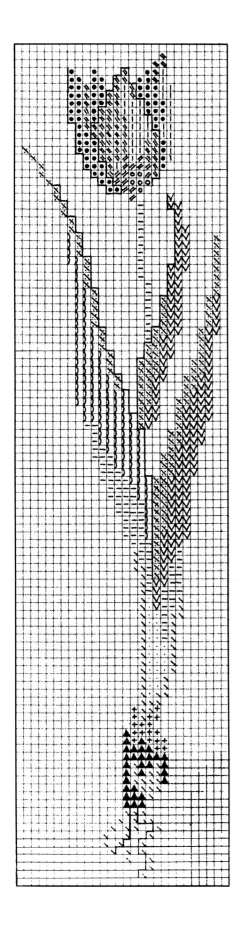

JACKET WITH TULIPS

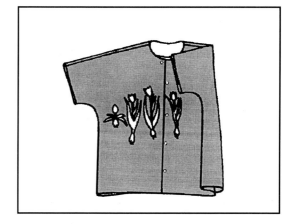

KEY TO CHARTS

		DMC				DMC
—	= light green	955		//	= orange	947
⊠	= green	905		○	= yellow	743
⊃	= apple green	704		⋅	= light yellow	745
V	= bright green	906		＼	= camel	738
		= strawberry	893		+	= brown	433
＼	= dark strawberry	891		▲	= dark brown	610
●	= red	349		■	= dark taupe	3021
▼	= dark red	816		⋅	= ecru	712

BACKPACK WITH FLAGS

~

Materials

A piece of linen with 20 threads per inch (2.5 cm); DMC embroidery floss as indicated on the chart for the flag sampler; a purchased backpack.

Directions

Cut a piece of linen large enough to cover the area where you want to place the flags. Pin the linen in position. Embroider the motif in cross stitch, using four strands of floss over two threads. Unravel the unembroidered linen and trim away the excess.

Also shown on page 2.

KEY TO CHART

			DMC
·	=	white	white
—	=	yellow	444
O	=	light brown	436
X	=	red	666
V	=	dark red	815
∴	=	light blue	828
L	=	light turquoise	996
+	=	turquoise	995
●	=	blue	820
\	=	green	911
■	=	black	310

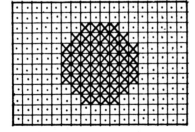

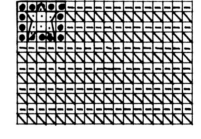

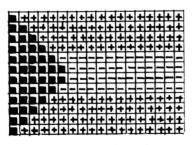

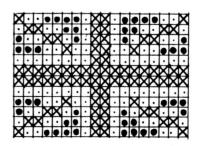

CHRISTMAS BIB

✂ Finished Measurements
9" x 10-1/2" (23 x 26.5 cm)

Materials

11-3/4" x 13-3/4" (30 x 35 cm) of white Aida cloth with 11 thread groups per inch (2.5 cm); the same size piece of white flannel; DMC or Anchor embroidery floss as indicated on the chart; 2 yds (1.75 m) of red seam binding 3/4" (2 cm) wide; basting thread; red sewing thread.

Directions

Using the sketch as a guide, make a paper pattern and use it to cut out a piece of Aida cloth. Embroider the motif following the chart, using three strands of floss and working each cross stitch over one thread group. Place Santa in the center, 1" from the lower edge. Embroider the red star motifs along each edge. Place the second star motif 11 thread groups above the first and spaced two thread groups closer to center. Work the third motif 11 thread groups above the second and five thread groups closer to the center than the first. For the stem stitches, use two strands of black floss

Cut a piece of flannel the same size as the Aida cloth. Place the pieces wrong sides together and sew the red seam binding around the bib, starting at one side of the neck and ending at the other side. Center a second piece of red seam binding at the center of the neck and sew the binding to the neck, leaving long tails at each end for ties.

KEY TO CHART

		DMC	Anchor
·	= white	white	1
●	= black	310	403
X	= red	666	46
◣	= dark green	699	923
◿	= green	702	226
⌣	= flesh	951	778
I	= pink	956	40
◹	= light pink	957	26
+	= orange yellow	972	303

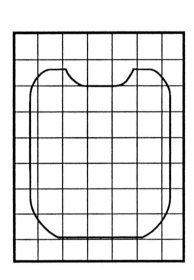

PATTERN FOR BIB

1 square = 1-1/2" (4 cm)

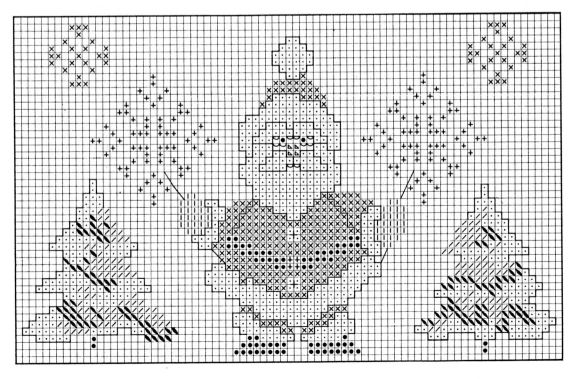

113

BLOUSE WITH PINK AND YELLOW FLOWERS

~

Materials

Blouse pattern; white Hardanger cloth with 22 double threads per inch (2.5 cm); DMC embroidery floss as indicated on the chart.

Directions

Purchase a pattern for a slipover blouse with a plain front and full, peasant-style sleeves. The blouse should not open down the front. The simpler the style, the more prominent the cross-stitched flowers will be. Make the blouse from white Hardanger cloth.

Work the large floral motif at center front of blouse. Work it a second time directly underneath the first motif. Place the left motif on the chart at the center of the right sleeve; place the right motif at the center of the left sleeve. Use two strands of floss over two double threads, beginning embroidery at point A. Begin sleeve embroidery 10" (25.5 cm) from lower edge. Working each stitch over two double threads, add rows of pink cross stitch along the lower edge of the sleeves and the edge of the neck.

KEY TO CHART

		DMC
− =	moss green	3348
V =	green	701
∴ =	pale green	369
I =	light green	966
L =	yellow green	703
Z =	spruce	320
⊥ =	grass green	909
● =	red	326
X =	strawberry	892
+ =	pink	3326
∷ =	bright yellow	726
⌐ =	light yellow	3078
· =	pale yellow	746
∧ =	yellow	727
O =	orange	742

JEANS WITH BICYCLE

~

Materials

Denim bib overalls; even-weave linen fabric with 19 threads per inch (2.5 cm); DMC embroidery floss as indicated on the chart.

Directions

Cut a piece of linen large enough for the motif. Count the threads on the linen to be sure that there are enough threads to embroider the motif. Pin the piece of linen to the front of the jeans. (If desired, remove the pocket from the overalls to make the embroidery easier.) Center the motif and work it in cross stitch, using two strands of floss over one thread. Stem stitch the mouths in red, along the outline of the socks in pink or dark blue, and around the blue bow in blue. Embroider the eyes in dark blue French knots. When the motif is complete, unravel the unembroidered linen and trim away the excess.

KEY TO CHART		
		DMC
· =	flesh	948
· =	light pink	819
:: =	pink	776
X =	dark pink	899
O =	lilac	604
■ =	red	666
/ =	yellow	973
v =	brown	402
= =	green	702
— =	light blue	827
V =	blue	813
● =	dark blue	996

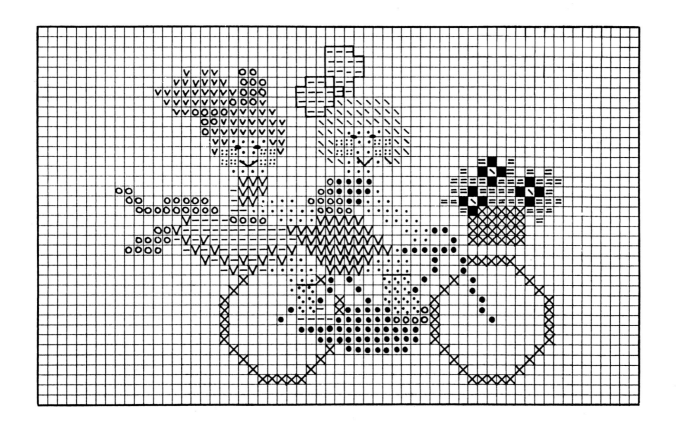

APRON

~

Materials

10" x 28" (25 x 70 cm) of white Hardanger fabric with 22 double threads per inch (2.5 cm); blue #820 DMC embroidery floss; 1 yd x 60" (0.85 m x 150 cm) of white cotton.

Directions

From the Hardanger cloth, cut two pieces 10" x 14" (25 x 30 cm) and two pieces 8" x 10" (20 x 25 cm). Mark the vertical and horizontal centers of a large piece and center the chart at point M on one long side. (The long sides will be the vertical edges of the finished apron bib.) Using two strands of floss, work each stitch over two double threads. Embroider the complete motif once, then turn the chart 180° and work from top to bottom to complete the other half of the bib. Cut 3/4" (2 cm) seam allowances outside the embroidered motif.

Mark a 6-3/4" x 7-1/2" (17 x 19 cm) rectangle on one of the small pieces of fabric. Mark the horizontal and vertical centers of the rectangle and embroider the motifs inside the rectangle. Select individual motifs from the chart and position them as shown in the photo. Embroider the upper border four double threads from the upper edge of the rectangle. Embroider the five motifs two double threads under the border, with the corner motifs five double threads from the side seams. Center one corner motif and center small motifs between the three corner motifs. Embroider the six small motifs beginning seven double threads from the side edges, and 10 double threads and 3-1/4" (8 cm) from the lower edge. Center the center row of motifs above the lower motifs. See photo. Trim rectangle to 1/4" (1 cm) outside the marked rectangle. Place the two pocket pieces right sides together and sew around three sides, leaving one side open for turning. Turn the pocket right side out and sew the opening closed.

For the apron skirt, cut a piece of fabric 24" x 26" (60 x 65 cm). For the waistband, cut out two strips 2" x 60" (5 x 150 cm). For the neck ties, cut out four strips 2" x 24" (5 x 60 cm). Place the neck ties right sides together; sew along long edges and one narrow edge. Turn right side out and sew the end closed. Make a second piece in the same manner. Place the embroidered bib and second 10" x 14" piece of Hardanger cloth right sides together and sew around three edges, leaving the lower edge open. Turn right side out. Sew the neck ties to each side of bib. Place the waistband strips right sides together and pin the bib to the center of one waist strip. Sew around the edges, leaving an opening 17-1/4" (43 cm) at the center of the lower edge. Make a 1/4" (1 cm) hem with inner hem on the lower edge. Sew on the pocket 10" (25 cm) from the lower edge and 2-1/2" (6 cm) from the side seam. Gather the top of the skirt to 17-1/4" and insert it in the waistband. Pin and sew along the edge.

KEY TO CHART

X̄ = blue

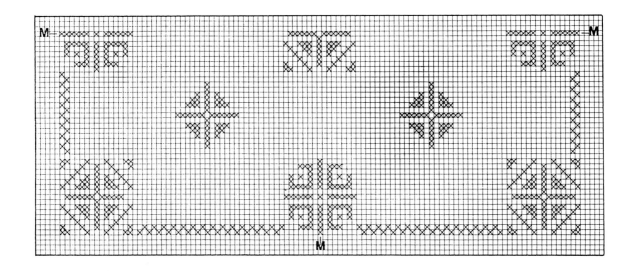

CHRISTMAS PAJAMAS

Materials

Child's red flannel pajamas; two 4" x 4" (10 x 10 cm) pieces of linen with 20 threads per inch (2.5 cm); DMC or Anchor embroidery floss as indicated on the chart.

Directions

Pin a piece of linen to the center of each pocket. Using three strands of floss, work each cross stitch over two threads, working through both thicknesses. Unravel the unembroidered linen and trim away the excess.

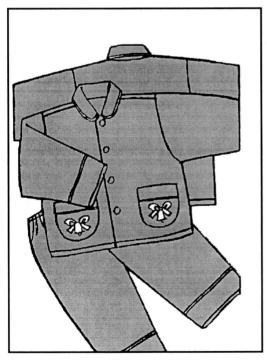

KEY TO CHART

		DMC	Anchor
·	= white	white	1
●	= green	699	923
X	= light green	702	227
\	= orange	741	314
—	= yellow	973	297

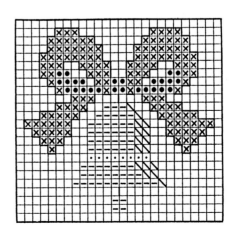

BIKER SHIRT

~

Materials

Strip of Hardanger cloth 2-1/2" (6 cm) wide and 1 yd (0.9 m) long, or the same length as the circumference of the T-shirt plus 1/2" (1.5 cm), with 25 double threads per inch (2.5 cm); DMC embroidery floss as indicated on the chart.

Directions

Embroider the motif in cross stitch by following the chart. Using three strands of floss, work each cross stitch over two double threads. Embroider the stem stitches in black. Embroider the biker motifs across the strip, working to the desired length. Hem the edges and sew the band around the T-shirt 1/4" (1 cm) under the sleeves. Sew up the ends of the band.

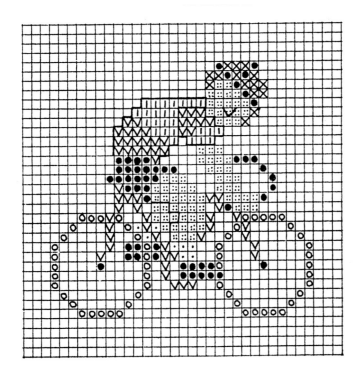

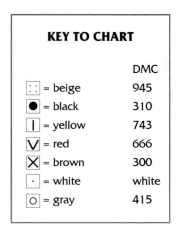

KEY TO CHART

		DMC
∷	= beige	945
●	= black	310
I	= yellow	743
V	= red	666
X	= brown	300
·	= white	white
O	= gray	415

FANNY PACK

~

✂ Finished Measurements
6" x 10" (15 x 25 cm)

Materials
10-3/4" x 12-3/4" (27 x 32 cm) of red even-weave fabric with 19 threads per inch (2.5 cm); DMC embroidery floss as indicated on the chart; a blue 10" (25 cm) long zipper; elastic 1-1/4" (3 cm) wide; a buckle.

Directions
Cut a piece of red fabric 7-1/2" x 10-3/4" (19 x 27 cm) and a piece 5-3/4" x 10-3/4" (14.5 x 27 cm). Embroider the small piece in cross stitch, following the chart and centering the motif. Using one strand of floss, work each stitch over two threads. Use three strands of black for the stem stitches.

Fold under 1/4" (1 cm) of the top edge of the embroidered piece and

1/4" of one long edge of the large piece of red fabric. Sew the zipper to these two pieces.

Cut two identical-size pieces of elastic. Fold the red fabric in half, right sides together, and pin each piece of

elastic to the top of the pack on the wrong side. Sew along the lower and side edges of the pack through all thicknesses. Attach a buckle at end of the elastic. Unzip the pack and turn it right side out.

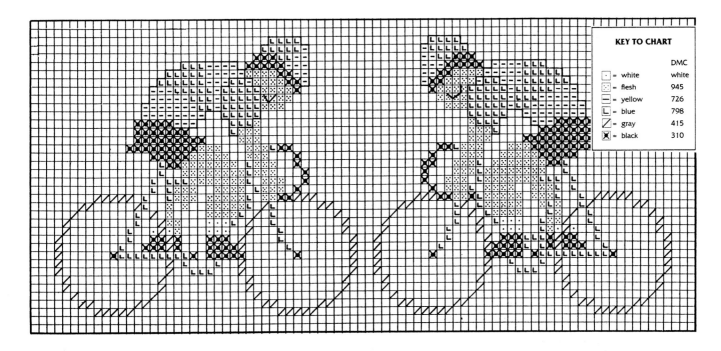

KEY TO CHART

		DMC
· = white	white
= flesh	945
− = yellow	726
L = blue	798
/ = gray	415
X = black	310

BLOUSE WITH FOLK ART MOTIF

~

✂ **Size**
Medium

Materials

1-1/2 yds (1.35 m) black cotton 56"
(140 cm) wide; DMC embroidery floss
as indicated on the chart; 42" (1.05 m)
black cotton cord.

Directions

Make a paper pattern of the pattern
pieces by following the graph. Note
center fold lines and place all pieces
on doubled fabric. Cut out the pieces.

Embroider the motif in cross stitch,
following the chart. Use two strands of
floss over two threads. Begin the front
motif at point M, exactly at the center

Chart for Front

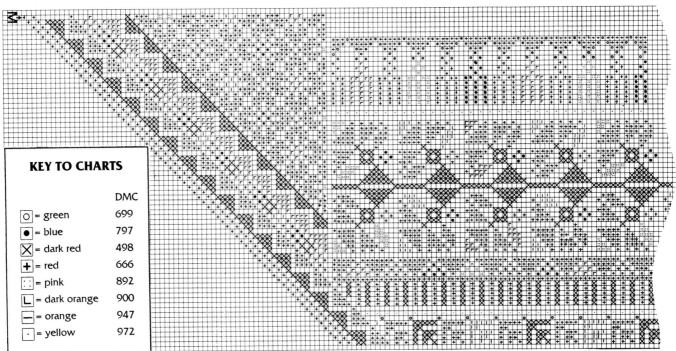

KEY TO CHARTS		
		DMC
O = green		699
● = blue		797
X = dark red		498
+ = red		666
⸭ = pink		892
L = dark orange		900
− = orange		947
· = yellow		972

fold line and 10" (25 cm) from the neck. Reverse the motif for the right half of the blouse. Embroider the sleeves, placing the motif at the center. Cut out the fabric with 1/4" (1 cm) seam allowances and with 3/4" (2 cm) hems. Cut out one piece of neck facing from black fabric with 1/4" seam allowances. Sew the shoulder seams together. Sew the sleeve seams, then sew the sleeves to the body. Sew back neck facing to back. Cut the center front to 1/4" above embroidery. Sew front facing and turn to inside. Sew facing seams. Cut two pieces of cord and wrap ends with red and yellow floss as shown in photo. Make a hem along lower edges of blouse and sleeves.

Chart for Sleeve

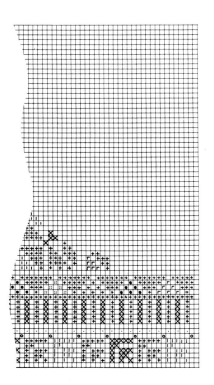

Pattern for Blouse
1 square = 1-1/2" (4 cm)

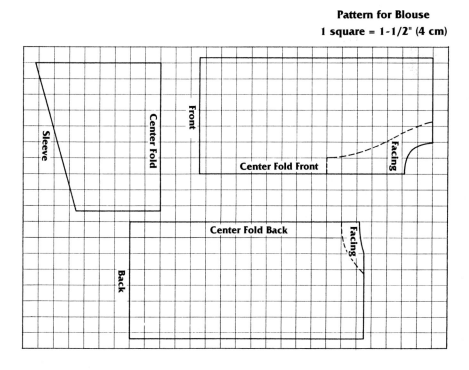

Sleeve

Center Fold

Front

Center Fold Front

Facing

Center Fold Back

Facing

Back

Skirt and Matching Bag

～

Skirt

Materials

2 yds (1.6 m) of red cotton fabric with 25 threads per inch (2.5 cm); DMC embroidery floss as indicated on the chart; fusible interfacing for the waistband; 7" (18 cm) zipper; hook and eye.

Directions

The measurements—for example, the length of the waistband—should be modified to fit the wearer. Another alternative is to purchase a pattern for a simple gathered skirt that is the correct size. The measurements given here should fit a medium-small woman.

Cut two pieces of red fabric 52" x 29-1/4" (130 x 73 cm). For the waistband cut a strip 28-3/4" x 4" (72 x 10 cm). Embroider the motif in cross stitch along a long edge of a large red cotton piece. Work each cross stitch using three strands of floss over three threads, following the chart. Begin the embroidery 2-1/2" (6 cm) from the lower edge (a long edge) and 1/2" (1.5 cm) from the right edge. Embroider the border to a width of 49-1/2" (124 cm). Embroider the second piece of red cotton in the same way.

Embroider the waistband with a blue border and a motif 2-1/4" (5.5 cm) from the long edge and 1/4" (1 cm) from a short edge. Work the motif along the entire length of the waistband. Right sides together, sew the side seams of the skirt together with a 1/4" seam allowance, leaving 7-1/2" (19 cm) open at the top of the left seam for the zipper. Press the seams open and sew in the zipper, leaving 3/4" (2 cm) open at the top.

Gather the top of the skirt to fit.

Cut a piece of fusible interfacing to fit the waistband and iron the interfacing to the wrong side of the waistband. Right sides together, sew the waistband to the top of the skirt. Fold the waistband in half to the inside and hem in place. Hem the skirt. Sew on the hook and eye above the zipper.

Bag

Materials

24" x 20" (60 x 50 cm) piece of red cotton fabric with 25 threads per inch (2.5 cm); DMC embroidery floss as indicated on the chart; 23" x 20" (58 x 50 cm) piece of black cotton fabric for lining; small piece of black cotton for the bottom of the bag; 9 plastic rings 3/4" (2 cm) in diameter; 1-1/2 yd (1.25 m) of black cord.

Directions

Cut a piece of red cotton 24" x 12" (60 x 30 cm). For the bottom, cut a 7-1/2" (19 cm) diameter circle of red cotton. Embroider the motif in cross stitch, following the chart. Work each cross stitch over three threads, using three strands of floss. Begin the embroidery with three black cross stitches 1-1/2" (4 cm) from the lower edge (a long edge) and 1-1/4" (3 cm) from the right edge. Repeat the motif across to the left edge. Begin the upper motif 42 threads from the top flower of the lower motif. Fold the embroidered piece in half, right sides together, and sew the short ends together with a 3/4" (2 cm) seam allowance. Line the red fabric circle with fusible interfacing. Sew the circular bottom to the

bag with 1/4" (1 cm) seam allowance. Turn the bag right side out. Two threads from the upper edge of the embroidery, fold the fabric to the inside and slip stitch in place. *Lining:* Cut a piece of black cotton 23" x 11-1/2" (58 x 29 cm). For the bottom, cut a 7-1/2" diameter circle. Fold the large piece right sides together and sew the short ends to form a ring. Sew the bottom to the ring. Fold the top 2-1/2" (6 cm) to the outside. Insert the lining in the bag and sew the top of the lining in place. Sew the plastic rings 1-1/4" from the upper edge, beginning 1" (2.5 cm) from the seam, and space them evenly around. Trim red fabric from inside ring, fold black fabric over ring, and embroider around the rings using black embroidery floss in satin stitch. Thread the cord through the rings.

Skirt Motif

KEY TO CHARTS

		DMC
O	= gray	318
+	= yellow	307
●	= black	310
V	= blue	517
X	= brown	839

Purse Motif

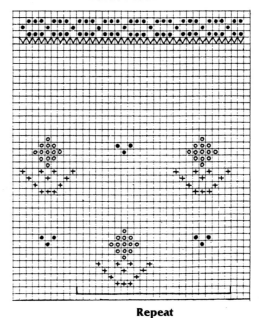

Repeat

INDEX

~